God, Self & Community

REVELATION, TESTIMONY & PRACTICE

God, Self & Community

REVELATION, TESTIMONY & PRACTICE

Dr. Bernard L. Brookes

BHM International, Inc.
North Potomac, Maryland

BHM INTERNATIONAL, INC.

We Support Being, Health, and Meaning through Publishing, Consultation, and Training

Published by BHM International, Inc.
14905-A Damson Terrace
North Potomac, Maryland
301-330-2717
www.bhm.com

ISBN 0-9741344-0-6

Library of Congress Control Number: 2003092947

To my wife Glenda,
and our grandchildren Jasmyne and Diamond,
who have taught me how to see everything again
through the eyes of a child

CONTENTS

ACKNOWLEDGMENTS

I want to thank Pastor Joseph Austin, the Rev. Janice Austin, and all of the members of Poplar Grove Baptist Church for welcoming my family and me to their community. They have provided us with the opportunity for Christian fellowship, spiritual development, and shared responsibilities. My wife, Glenda Brookes, has been supportive in many ways, including listening to me read aloud some book sections soon after I had written them. The spoken word, shared between lifetime companions, creates a reality of both confirmation and correction that does not come from the reverberation of words in the mind and on the page. My sisters, Dr. Marilane Bond and Francene Roberts, in sharing their reactions to the book section about our mother, gave me valuable feedback on the authenticity of what I tried to express. Oumie Joof, my business assistant and organizer, was helpful in the practical tasks such as proofreading and office management. As a Muslim, she also helped me to keep in mind the different doorways that humanity has to finding God.

Many writers, from the biblical prophets and the apostles, to modern theologians, psychologists, scientists, and other seekers, have provided companionship and guidance through their written testimonies of their experiences wrestling with or studying good and evil, wisdom and ignorance, and all the other issues connected to meaning and value for human beings. One with whom I actually had contact by e-mail was Laurie Beth Jones, author of *Jesus, CEO* and *Jesus, Inc.* I was moved in reading in the latter book about how her life was transformed when she seemed to have reached a dead end on the path she had previously followed. She responded to my e-mail and gave me encouragement and helpful suggestions. I would also like to mention the groundbreaking work of Dr. M. Scott Peck, author of *The Road Less Traveled* and several other books, for helping to integrate spirituality with psychology and psychiatry in the public mind, as well as with the professional disciplines.

While those mentioned above, and others, have inspired or supported me in writing this book, they are not responsible for the views expressed in it, and the manner in which they are expressed. In fact, I'm certain that some of them would not agree with some of my specific positions and ideas. I take full responsibility for the contents of this book, while accepting their unconditional love and support.

INTRODUCTION

> *"Every [person] lives in two realms, the internal and the external. The internal is that realm of spiritual ends expressed in art, literature, morals, and religion. The external is that complex of devices, techniques, mechanism, and instrumentalities by means of which we live . . . We have allowed the means by which we live to outdistance the ends for which we live . . . Enlarged material powers spell enlarged peril if there is not proportionate growth of the soul."*
> — MARTIN LUTHER KING JR.[1]

Sometimes spirit and community are seen as opposites, or mutually exclusive. Some people who focus on developing themselves and others spiritually become detached and removed from the problems and needs of the broader community and the world. They become self-absorbed, or absorbed in a false sense of self. At the other extreme, some people are totally focused on accomplishing things and having an effect on their community, in what they consider the "real" world, while they deny and ignore their own spiritual development and that of others. But this is a false dichotomy. Spirit, which is about the relationship of the self to the Creator, source of being, or God, and community, which is the relationship of the self to others, are two essential aspects of a health personality.

This book tells stories from my own personal development,

and discusses ideas from Christianity and from psychology that have been helpful in getting me on the path to becoming fully myself, everything God intended for me to be. James W. Fowler, a theologian who built upon the psychological theories of Jean Piaget, Erik Erikson, and Lawrence Kolberg in his research on stages of faith, writes about the triadic shape of the covenantal relationship between self, others, and "shared centers of value and power" that are essential to the development of self and community.[2] God, self, and community are, in my view, the three points on that triad and are the three central concepts providing coherence to this book. Three secondary concepts that I have found helpful are revelation, testimony, and practice.

Psychologists usually talk more about other people, their patients, or research subjects, than about their own personal development and experiences. Spiritual concepts such as revelation and testimony, and even discussion of God, are also not usually comfortable areas for psychologists; for by training we are social scientists who are taught to stay within the realm of thought, feeling, and behavior that can be expressed in ways that are observable and measurable (though there is movement within psychology to recognize the reality, and the healthy effects, of spiritual life[3]). As a group, we would probably find the concept of "practice" familiar—a basic idea indicating that knowledge is incorporated into behavior through repetition, rehearsal, and social reinforcement.

I believe that full development of the self requires revelation, which is any experience of what theologian Paul Tillich calls "ultimate concern" or "the power of that which is holy and which therefore has an unconditional claim on us."[4] More simply, it is an experience that brings us face to face with the reality that there is more to our lives than material existence. This is usually understood as spirit and, in Christianity, as God manifesting as the Holy Spirit; and in the "original revelation" of Jesus as the

Christ. Each religion is a doorway to God, but no religion owns or controls God. Each religion provides a symbolic system of meaning based on particular histories and cultural practices evolved from a people's experience of God. Believers today experience God as living and not just an abstract concept through the personal connection of their own internal and external lives with the religious system that has meaning for them.

Without religion, the experience of spiritual transformation is reduced to abstract moral principles, without vitality and life. Each religion provides the stories, songs, symbols, and rituals that enable the faithful in the present to experience God as alive through the link back to the original revelation by the founder, prophet, or God incarnate. However, the claim of any religion to exclusive truth is more likely the expression of an egoistic, chauvinistic, or tribal impulse than of Godly humility and love. True spiritual leadership and maturity is expressed by living the example of faith and love, not through fomenting religious intolerance.

Jesus defined the essential issues involved in being in relationship with God when he reduced the Judaic ten commandments to two underlying ones: Love God above all else, and love your neighbor as yourself. To love God above all else means to recognize that our spiritual and moral being, which we experience as real through the God relationship, is more valuable to the integrity of our self, community, and world, than all the material benefits of life, or even physical life itself. Not that we need to repudiate the reality or importance of physical life, but that we strive to order our lives in the material world, according to the spiritual and moral purpose we experience through connection with God, the source of being and creativity. Then secondly, it follows empathically that we regard our fellow human beings as God's children like ourselves, and love them as we love ourselves.

It is likely that every religion has these two elements it its foundation. The rest is history, tradition, and doctrine, which are important in creating the symbolic world in which the self apprehends God through revelation, but which does not in truth require us to deny that there are other doorways to God. Fundamentalism of every religious type reverses the importance of these elements of faith. Doctrine becomes more important than loving God or loving other human beings. This inevitably leads to religious hatred and the repudiation of the essential truthfulness of every other faith but one's own. If we focus instead on loving God and loving other human beings, the result is empathy and connection with others based on these principles.

Only those who are primarily Machiavellian and predatory in outlook would disagree with the principle of treating others as you would like to be treated, of developing the capability for empathy (not just sympathy), of being able to truly understand and appreciate the perspectives and experiences of other human beings, and to act with their interests in mind as well as one's own. But the principle about loving God above all else really gives some people difficulty. They will ask: why do we need this God whom we cannot see, and whose existence we cannot verify? We answer that the God relationship is experienced through revelation and faith, which, with spiritual practice, transform our persons and our lives. We testify that there is a joy and strength that comes with a relationship to God that enables us to become fully ourselves, and to endure and overcome the world. But until they begin looking inward and developing a spiritual life, our words and expressions cannot convey to them the true meaning of our experience.

Revelation cannot be experienced as an abstract concept. It occurs within the context of one's particular life and community. It is important to understand that revelation does not always come as a blinding light that knocks you off your horse, as it did with the apostle Paul. It can come in a simple moment sitting on the porch with one's children, or listening to music, or in prayer or meditation. The monk and author Thomas Merton wrote: "Every moment and every event of every [person's] life on earth plants something in [the] soul. For just as the wind carries thousands of winged seeds, so each moment brings with it germs of spiritual vitality that come to rest imperceptibly in the minds and wills of [human beings]."[5]

Testimony follows revelation inevitably, for we become ourselves through interaction with other human beings. When we experience something as profound, meaningful, and joyful as revelation, we must tell others about it. That is how original revelations, such as Jesus as the Christ, spread and became institutional religions. Despite life-threatening obstacles, the experience is too powerful to suppress. That desire and need to testify continues today. "In testimony, a believer describes what God has done in her life, in words both biblical and personal, and the hands of her friends clap in affirmation. Her individual speech thus becomes part of an affirmation that is shared."[6] This book is part of my testimony and is expressed in the languages I know: personal stories, the language of psychology and self-development, and the language of Christian faith.

Testimony is also an expression of our own creativity, and of our connection with its source, the Creator. Testimony is at times no more coherent than a shout of joy or the uncontrollable flowing of tears of gratitude, as we realize how precious is the gift of life and of love with which we have been blessed. Our music, not just religious music, and the other arts are expressions of experiences of creativity and the Creator. Paul Tillich writes: "From the point of view of the creature, the purpose of creation is the creature itself and the actualization of its potentialities. From the point of view of the creator, the purpose of creation is the exercise of his creativity, which has no purpose beyond itself because the divine life is essentially creative."[7] In my life, music has been an important part of revelation and testimony, and in this book, I relate and discuss some of those experiences.

After experiencing revelation and testimony, a person must practice the new ways of living in order to actually develop and move toward becoming fully oneself in the context of one's community. That is the truly difficult task. For it usually means making major changes in one's life. It is similar to what a person faces who wants to free himself from a serious addiction. He has to change the people with whom he spends time, the places he goes, and the types of activities he engages in. A significant part of practice is developing a social support network that reinforces the behaviors and attitudes of the new lifestyle.

Christianity provides a community and social network in which to practice the new behaviors consistent with a "transformed mind." It is called church. Unfortunately, church today is sometimes a calcified remnant of the original revelation experience, with dogmatic approaches that are inconsistent with experiencing revelation and full development of self and community in the twenty-first century. I have found it possible to become an active participant in a church community, in a way that is vital and personally satisfying. But this has required that I do much of the serious spiritual study on my own, so that when I joyfully participate in church service, my mind as well as my spirit says amen.

It seems that American churches, such as African-American Protestant and white evangelical churches, which focus on enabling worshippers to have an ecstatic and immediately personal relationship with God through experience of the Holy Spirit, also tend to be literalist and fundamental in their interpretation of the Bible. Literalist interpretations of the Bible will inevitably conflict with scientific knowledge for a nondogmatic twenty-first century person. Some people can accept these contradictions without apparent problems. But for others, it causes spiritual life to remain alienated from, rather than becoming integrated into, daily life. This can actually undermine faith and encourage duplicity.

The need for moral and spiritual community is real, and despite the limitations of the church, temple, mosque, or other place of worship, it is the place where most people must go to help build communities of faith. Others will build spiritual communities outside of organized religion, and that is also to be encouraged. However, most of humanity will have to struggle to find meaning and renewal in our traditional faiths. In doing so, we should recognize that to be successful, we must each bring some creative energy and willingness to do the necessary individual and family spiritual study and practice outside of the sanctuary. Secondly, it is important to select a spiritual community in which one can connect empathically with the leadership and body as a whole. Finally, practicing the message of humility helps to keep the ego in check, and enables us to learn from others with different perspectives and experiences.

The action component of revelation, and specifically in Christian revelation, is the commandment to love God above all else and to love each other as we love ourselves. This simple demand becomes a challenging task when we acknowledge the reality of our social situation. It is not just a private matter of our individual salvation and self-development. From psychology, as well as from the common sense experience of raising children, we know that the self develops in relation to others. And there can therefore be no self-actualization that an individual obtains like a high from alcohol or other drugs. As theologian Rheinhold Niebuhr states, "Community is an individual as well as social necessity; for the individual can realize himself only in intimate and organic relation with his fellowmen. Love is therefore the primary law of his nature, and brotherhood the fundamental requirement of his social existence."[8]

We now live in a global society, whose economic and social foundations were built on African slavery, the decimation of indigenous people in the Americas and elsewhere, the colonization of Asia and Africa, and the sinful exploitation everywhere of the poor by the rich, of women by men, and of the earth by human beings. Fifty years ago, white male Christians of the middle class or the wealthy could say their prayers, worship in church, be kind to their family and neighbors—and ignore their complicity in this world of sin.

Today, all that has changed, at least in our global understanding of right and wrong. As a world, we acknowledge the standard of universal human rights, gender equality, racial equality, the need to conserve the earth's resources, and the responsibility to alleviate poverty and suffering. The escapist route is to quickly acknowledge the sins of the past, to declare that we now all have equal opportunity, and to get back to the business of accumulating goods and services for ourselves and our loved ones. Another avenue for the escapist is to pursue our salvation and that of others in the spiritual world, while neglecting suffering and injustice in the physical world.

The path to full development of self and community involves revelation, testimony, and practice in this world. It requires facing the threat of being overwhelmed by our apparent powerlessness to change even our own behavior; never mind changing the world with its billions of people and its conflicts, injustice, and suffering. Pride, anger, fear, and greed seem to drown out the music of love and humility in our own personal interactions, as well as in the global interaction of nations and business organizations. To find the courage to hope, believe, struggle, and rejoice, without escapism, is the challenge today to our psychological health, our faith, our creativity, and our survival.

one

WE ARE EACH SPECIAL IN GOD'S SIGHT

> *"Therefore each particular being, in its individuality, its concrete nature and entity, with all its own characteristics and its private qualities and its own inviolable identity, gives glory to God by being precisely what He wants it to be here and now, in the circumstances ordained for it by His Love and His infinite Art. . . . Trees and animals have no problem. God makes them what they are without consulting them, and they are perfectly satisfied. With us it is different. God leaves us free to be whatever we like. We can be ourselves or not, as we please."*
> — THOMAS MERTON[1]

We Are Each Special in God's Sight

One day in 1950, on the Caribbean island of St. Kitts, my mother was pregnant with me, and her mother, who was dying, asked her to come close, saying "I won't harm your baby." It did not sound the way I am writing it, because she said it in the English patois that was my first language. Anyway, my grandmother said what she did because the local belief was that a person who is dying could, through the exercise of some sort of demonic power, harm

1

a baby in a mother's womb. So my mother, trusting her mother with my life, moved to my grandmother's side. My grandmother touched my mother's belly and said that I would be a special child. My mother told me this story when I was about thirty years old. She obviously believed my grandmother's prediction. She named me after the white doctor who delivered me and expected me to become a physician. Her belief was reinforced by the fact that I was academically gifted compared to my siblings and the other children around us, or perhaps it was the special expectations that was the cause of my gifts.

In some families, one child is seen as special. And even though the other children are also loved, that one child is viewed by the parents as having a special destiny. It may be because the child has some obvious special gifts or talents, or it may be something more difficult to define. In any event, there are consequences to all of the children because of this special selection. In my family, I was that special child. It may have been because I was the first child of my mother's second marriage, the one from which five of her seven children came. It may have also had something to do with being a male child. Or it may have been because of my grandmother's prediction.

In some ways, it is great to be considered special, but it can also mean bearing the psychological burden of feeling that you can never live up to the expectations placed on you. It also means struggling with your own ego against a tendency toward arrogance, the sin of pride. But it is probably the other children in the family who carry the heaviest burden. My older brother Leroy had particular difficulty within our family dynamic. To begin with, he was the only child from my mother's first marriage. And secondly, he had difficulty learning things that I found easy. Today, we would probably consider him learning disabled, but back then we didn't know about such things.

Being from the previous marriage, Leroy was already struggling with being the outsider, and his learning problems, in contrast to my academic success, solidified that position. Since he could not be good by the established family criteria, his identity became, to be bad. He was getting into trouble as far back as I could remember. And our relationship was an ambivalent one, with him being both my protector and tormentor. I was the thorn in his flesh because he could never get the positive attention that I did. My first memory of Leroy is from when I was about two or three years old. It is one of a small number of early memories, and I can date it approximately because at age three, I began attending a preschool. In this memory, which is like a brief film clip, my mother was bathing me in a tub in the backyard, and Leroy stood by laughing and making fun of me. But later, in many boyhood adventures, such as catching birds and lizards, I followed his lead like any younger brother follows his older brother.

The high point of my feeling of being special was when I graduated third in my high school class of over eight hundred, and got accepted to Harvard, Columbia, and other prestigious universities. But once I got out into the wider world of college, I quickly realized that there were many people more academically gifted and better educated than I. After that, I struggled with the conflicting desires to, on one hand, become significant in the world and, on the other, to get away from people and simply spend my time reading others' thoughts through their books, and wondering about life, death, and eternity.

My training and experience as a psychologist has helped. But it is through Christian study and prayer, that I finally have an understanding that we can each be special without it being at the expense of anyone else. Each of us has a unique gift—to become what only we can be, fully who we are, through an intimate relationship with God. In Christianity, that is made possible through the sacrifice of Jesus Christ; and through him, the working of the Holy Spirit in each person and in each person's life. "For you did not receive a spirit that makes you a slave again to fear, but you received the Spirit of sonship. And by him we cry, 'Abba, Father'. The Spirit himself testifies with our spirit that we are God's children. Now if we are children, then we are heirs—heirs of God and co-heirs with Christ, if indeed we share in his sufferings in order that we may also share in his glory."[2]

In the world, being special means in relation to other people, who are less special than you are. It is the ego crying out to be loved and accepted. But it is a child's ego, which believes that it alone must get the love of its mother. But in relation to God, each of us is special and loved, in a way that allows every other person to also be special and loved. But we cannot access God's love without giving up our selfish tendencies. Through his sacrifice, Jesus prepared the way. For Christians, he became the way by which we can have a personal relationship with God. But to get and maintain access, we must wage a lifetime war against our own fear and selfish desires. We must "Love the Lord your God with all your heart, and with all your soul and with all your mind and with all your strength." And we must "Love your neighbor as yourself."[3]

Keith, the Dime, and the Bastard
Who Could Not Get into Heaven

> *"A bastard shall not enter into the congregation of the Lord; even to his tenth generation shall he not enter into the congregation of the Lord."*
>
> — DEUTERONOMY 23:2[4]

I was about nine or ten years old when I met Keith. I don't remember how I came to know him, because he was not part of my regular circle of friends from school or church or the neighborhood, in my hometown of Basseterre, on the tiny Caribbean island of St. Kitts. What I do remember is that I lent Keith a dime, which at that time was for me a significant sum, considering that mother usually gave my older brother and me two cents each for church offering, of which we often spent one cent to buy candy on the way to church. I do not remember the circumstances under which I lent Keith the dime. In fact, I can only visualize two times when I was with Keith. In both situations, my feelings and perceptions were dominated by the desire to get my dime back from him.

In one of those two scenes, Keith and I were at Warner Park, where sports events (primarily soccer and cricket) were held. Sometimes they also had bicycle races, horse races, and other exhibitions. On this occasion, we were at a horse race, or perhaps it was bicycle racing. What I am certain of is that Keith and I were both there, sitting on the grass, and that he owed me a dime that I was trying to get him to repay.

Keith never did repay that dime, but he gave me a gift of sorts before he disappeared from my life. He gave me that "gift" the only other time I remember being with him. We were alone, sitting in my mother's room, and he offered to show me something. He took my mother's Bible and showed me Deuteronomy 23:2: "A bastard shall not enter into the congregation of the Lord; even to his tenth generation shall he not enter into the congregation of the Lord." I do not believe that Keith was motivated by the love of God when he showed me that passage. He had no doubt seen my parents' wedding picture hanging on our living room wall. In the photo, I was standing next to my mother and father. No, now that I think about it, Keith was no friend of mine.

Keith's "gift" was the first time that I experienced a direct connection between something written in the Bible and my own life, and it was disturbing. What I was being told was that because I was born out of wedlock, I could never go to heaven, no matter what I did in my life, and even my children and grandchildren could not go to heaven. I didn't think much about the children and grandchildren at that time, but it just seemed so unfair that I could never get into heaven, because of something over which I had no control.

At about that age, I spent a lot of time reading. I read just about anything I could get my hands on, and the Bible was one of the most readily available books in our house. Previously, I was drawn to the fascinating and mysterious stories about other people long ago and their interactions with God. I also enjoyed hearing the stories read in Sunday school and singing hymns assuring us that "Jesus loves the little children. All the children of the world, red and yellow, black and white, all are precious in his sight. Jesus loves the little children of the world." I was also struck by the story of when Samuel as a young boy was called by God. "The Lord came and stood there, calling as at the other times, 'Samuel! Samuel!' Then Samuel said, 'Speak, for your servant is listening.'"[5]

At that time, of course, I had no understanding of the difference between the Old Testament and the New Testament; that through his sacrifice, Jesus saves us by grace from the consequences of the law of the Old Testament. I certainly had no understanding of the difference between literal and symbolic interpretations of the Bible. To me, it was all the Bible and all unquestionable truth. I never asked anyone to help me solve this dilemma, probably because it was all too painful to my young mind. And so the seed of rebellion and distrust took root, and it would require a lifetime to unearth.

The Rock, the Rain, and Baptism in the Sea

> *"The rain came down, the streams rose, and the winds blew and beat against that house; yet it did not fall, because it had its foundation on the rock. But everyone who hears these words of mine and does not put them into practice is like a foolish man who built his house on sand. The rain came down, the streams rose, and the winds blew and beat against that house, and it fell with a great crash."*
>
> — MATTHEW 7: 25-27[6]

When I read in the Bible about the rock, I am brought back in memory to the large rock, a boulder, that sat in the front yard of our house on Fines Avenue in Basseterre. My older brother Leroy and I were drawn to that rock. It was a puzzle. And it resisted any attempts we made to move it. It seemed to serve absolutely no purpose, sitting there in the corner of the yard, near the concrete sidewalk, which went by at the height of about one foot above the level of our dirt yard. There was a small space between the rock and the sidewalk, and another small space between the rock and the adjacent fence, which separated our house and Mrs. Allen's next door.

In an alley, up the street in the opposite direction from the ocean front, were some men who did interesting things like practicing music as part of a steel band and lifting weights. There was one man in particular who was very muscular, and I often wondered if he could move the rock in our front yard. But I never had the occasion to ask him; and truth be told, children in St. Kitts were not in the habit of asking adults too much of anything. Both children and adults on St. Kitts agreed with the saying, "Children should be seen and not heard." This is alleged to be a Victorian saying, which found its way along with the British, and our slave ancestors, to our little island in the Caribbean.

But we did not feel particularly oppressed about having to stay out of the hearing of adults. In fact, we thrived on exploring the mysteries of our everyday surroundings on our own, within the boundaries and protection provided by our parents. Perhaps that's why it never occurred to me to ask my mother why the rock was in our front yard. We preferred to keep grappling with it, and fretting at it, than to have its mystery reduced to something as mundane as the laziness or oversight of the workers who constructed our basement. Besides, one always had to be careful of being hit by one of those profound and ominous sayings that older people used, when they thought children's play was getting out of bounds. One of these was "All skin teeth no laugh, just go to the burial ground and see!" which meant that the skeletons in the graveyard also grin, but the joke is on them.

Our house was not literally built on a rock; rather it had a concrete foundation. It was formerly a two-room wooden house, which was well and tightly built, like the wooden fishing boats that pulled up onto the sand down by the bay, where the fishermen would put up their scales and sell their fish right out of the boat, fresh from the ocean. At the time, I assumed that this was the way that everyone in the world bought fish. Originally, the wooden house was raised up off the ground, and the space underneath could be used for storing things or by me for exploring, when I was a very young child. But we had moved out of the Fines Avenue house for a few years to the Village, and during that time, the house was expanded for our growing family. While we were away in the Village, two brothers, Tony and Alfonso, were added to our existing trio, which consisted of my younger sister Marilane, my older brother Leroy, and myself.

The house was expanded by making a concrete basement, with windows on three sides, and two sets of steps leading up to doors in the rear. And for the first time, we had electric lights. So I could now read under an electric bulb, rather than near the oil lamps that we previously used. We still did not have running water, but this did not seem like a major lack, since many people around us had neither electricity nor running water. We simply went down the street each morning to the public pipe and "headed" water back home in containers.

There was only one front window in the basement, because the steps leading up to the front door on the main floor blocked the possibility of another basement window in the front. But that one window gave what was for us a great view onto the sidewalk and street, and old Miss Emily's house across the street.

One of the most interesting sights we saw through the front

window occurred during heavy rain. This was not the really heavy rain and wind, where the seas turned ugly; the hurricane rains and winds that folks like Ms. Libby down the road said tore the galvanized tin roofs from houses and sailed them through the air, sometimes chopping people's heads off. No, I'm not talking about that kind of heavy rain. I mean the kind of heavy rain that might start even when the sun was shining. And awful as it sounds today, when the rain fell while the sun remained shining, we children understood it to be because the devil was beating his wife with a ham bone.

But those rains were a happy occasion for the children next door. We were never allowed to do what they did. We could only watch with laughter, and some envy, as they ran up and down the sidewalk, naked in the rain. It was like some sort of liberating ritual that they practiced: running and laughing in the rain. Then the rain would stop, and life would go back to normal, and pretty soon we could go out also, but with our clothes on.

Another much more striking ritual would occasionally go past our house. This was a baptism in the sea. I don't know from which church the procession came. I assumed it was the small church just up the street and around the corner. A church we sometimes attended, the Church of God, was further down that same street, near the ice factory. Sometimes we looked in at the people in service in the small church as we walked to the Church of God.

Once in a while, the members of that church would suddenly appear in a procession, all dressed in white gowns, marching and singing past our house down to the sea. We would not get too close, because what they were doing, though strange to us, seemed powerful and important. We would just watch as they went by our house, then look down the long hill after them as they were baptized in the ocean.

I had seen christenings, which were performed when one is a child, in our primary church, the Moravian Church, but I had not observed adult baptism. In fact, the only similar experience I had was when, at almost the exact same location on the shore, my father threw me into the ocean in a misguided attempt to teach me to swim. It was a terrifying experience and made it difficult for me to learn to swim later on. As a result, although I lived about a block from the ocean in St. Kitts, I did not learn to swim until I went to the indoor pool at the YMCA in Mount Vernon, New York.

No, our house was not literally built on a rock, but our family was built on a rock. And that rock was my mother, from whom we imbibed, without fully understanding it, an almost instinctual appreciation of the importance of God in our lives, and the limitations and vulnerability of human beings. Her three marriages and the emotional instability of my father and stepfather certainly created some apprehension about the fragility and potential destructiveness of marital relationships, but she knew Jesus as the rock of her salvation. We thought that she was the rock. But she knew who was the true rock.

Knowledge Is Power

"Knowledge is power." — FRANCIS BACON[7]

"The fear of the Lord is the beginning of knowledge, but fools despise wisdom and discipline."
— PROVERBS 1:7[8]

The Irish Town School was not far from our house in Basseterre. The school was named after the neighborhood, not the road. Irish Town Road crossed Fines Avenue three houses from ours, just down the hill going toward the ocean. The two liquor stores, one on each corner of Fines Avenue and Irish Town Road, had jukeboxes that broadcast an almost constant stream of calypso music to our house and the neighborhood. The school was actually past Irish Town Road, set in an alley between Fines Avenue and the next street over. That next street had, instead of a hill like our street, a set of rounded stone stairs as wide as the street, narrowing a bit at the top, with a stone railing on both sides, which served as a barrier for the road above. And you could lean over the stone rail on Irish Town Road and look down about twenty feet to the bottom of the stairs and the street below. Once you got down that stair, it was a straight walk of half a block to the door of Irish Town School. Or you could go down the hill of Fines Avenue then turn right onto the alley.

The school itself was a large one-room building with a high ceiling. There were wooden benches with attached tables, which served as desks, grouped around the building for the different classes. The highest grade (approximately sixth grade) sat on a platform at the end of the building, which became a stage when the building was used on some Sundays for our Christmas and other holiday plays. The principal also had his desk on the stage, and occasionally, he would stand and address the entire school with a tough question, such as how to spell "colonel."

High up on the wall, perhaps forty feet above our heads, a phrase was inscribed on the wall in large letters. It said, " Knowledge is power." And I truly believed it. That phrase would echo in my head for the rest of my life, yet it is only recently that I bothered to find out its origin. I, and perhaps the rest of my fellow students of many generations, took it as an absolute truth. How could we believe otherwise, since it was inscribed with such majesty way above our heads? How could we even question it? The statement contains a certain intellectual arrogance and a promise of horizons without limits that became part of my developing self.

Only much later after bumping my head against the rocks of life, and of middle age, did I learn that "fear of God is the beginning of knowledge." The purpose of faith is not to provide an alternative scientific explanation of the material world. Science does a much better job of that, and the attempt of religion to compete on that ground is a futile attempt to fight a war that was lost long ago. Rather, the purpose of faith is to develop the spiritual aspects of humanity, without which we are likely to destroy ourselves and our world with our scientific knowledge and advancements.

We are not just organic computers in search of a mathematical solution. We are also spiritual beings searching for meaning and purpose in our lives. The fact that love is not a scientific concept does not make it any less meaningful to us as human beings.

Some talk of the merging of science and religion as physicists have realized the paradoxical nature of matter and energy at the subatomic level. We have come to realize that science is its own religion, with assumptions and beliefs that cannot be proven.[9] Ultimately, we cannot avoid the use of judgment in applying either scientific or spiritual knowledge.

To Kill a Sparrow

> *"Are not five sparrows sold for two copper coins? And not one of them is forgotten before God. But the very hairs of your head are still numbered. Do not fear therefore; you are of more value than many sparrows."*
>
> — LUKE 12:6-7[10]

As a small boy of nine on the island of St. Kitts, money was scarce, and we children were resourceful in making toys out of whatever scrap material we found lying around. We used to make a slingshot out of a forked twig from a tree and rubber cut from an old inner tube. Someone even developed a slingshot that could be aimed and released like a gun. Once I saw this slingshot gun, I knew I could make one and proceeded to do so. The wooden gun had a wire trigger, which, when pulled, lifted a circular piece of wire from a nail posted on the top of the wood toward the rear of the gun. The circular piece of wire was attached to the middle of a strip of rubber, the ends of which were attached to the front end of the gun.

I felt such boyish pride in my completed product. It worked perfectly as expected. The yard next to ours had trees and bushes in the back. One tree, which was right next to the fence, was a plant that produced hard round fruit, about one-half inch in diameter, which I later learned were poisonous. We regularly tossed those around, but had the sense not to put them in our mouth. They smelled awful in any case, so we had no interest in them as a source of food, even though we were at times hungry. In addition to that large tree, there were some smaller ones further away from the fence, in the middle of the yard next door. And that is where the sparrow landed.

We were fascinated by the birds that visited the one large tree in our backyard, which grew over the top of our outdoor kitchen. The kitchen was a small box-shaped shed, perhaps three-fourths the size of today's one-car garages, and made of corrugated tin, the material then used on most roofs in St. Kitts. The one large tree was next to the shed in the rear and seemed to grow right out of it, when viewed from the front. I would follow the lead of my older brother in setting traps to catch the birds on the roof of the kitchen shed. That activity, driven by curiosity and at times hunger, did not bother me emotionally. For that reason, my reaction to the results of using the gun I created was surprising.

So there I was, excited about having ingeniously created this weapon and impatient to try it out on a live target. Just then, a sparrow, or a small bird similar to a sparrow, landed on the small tree in the back of our neighbor's yard. I could see it clearly through the fence. I put a piece of lead in my gun and set it by stretching the rubber back until its wire connector was seated on the headless nail on the top rear of the gun, behind the trigger. I cautiously moved in until I was opposite my prey across the fence, aimed, and, without hesitation, fired. The sparrow fell to the ground dead.

What I experienced next was totally unexpected. I felt an overwhelming sense of guilt and remorse for what I had done and vowed never to kill another animal for sport again. I had expected to feel pride and a sense of accomplishment, but instead I felt remorse. I did not feel fear, as if expecting punishment from my parents, or from God. I just felt that I had done something wrong. I understood, for the first time, that living things have intrinsic value and are sacred. We can kill and eat them when we are hungry, but they are not ours to destroy for pleasure, or to demonstrate our own cleverness and ingenuity.

The Stoning and Shunning

> *"The teachers of the law and the Pharisees brought in a woman caught in adultery. They made her stand before the group and said to Jesus, 'Teacher, this woman was caught in the act of adultery. In the Law Moses commanded us to stone such women. Now what do you say?' They were using this question as a trap, in order to have a basis for accusing him. But Jesus bent down and started to write on the ground with his finger. When they kept on questioning him, he straightened up and said to them, 'If any one of you is without sin, let him be the first to throw a stone at her.'"*
>
> — JOHN 8:3-7[11]

Our house on Fines Avenue in the Irish Town Neighborhood of Basseterre on the island of St. Kitts was owned by my mother, who had inherited it from her mother; but the land on which it stood belonged to someone else, to whom we paid rent. I don't know whether that was an unusual or common arrangement, but that is how it was. We lived in that house from my birth until I was about three. At that time our house had two rooms, was made of wood, and was raised off the ground. I can remember playing underneath it, but keeping some distance from our dog, who was

14

fierce and who was tied up at one corner under the house.

We moved out of the Fines Avenue house to the Village for about four years, and two of my bothers were born there. When we returned to the Fines Avenue house, a finished basement had been built with one window facing the street, two on the left side, and one on the right. Two parallel sets of cement steps, which together spanned the width of the house were separated by a cement wall, and each led up from the back of the basement through a separate door to the backyard. The stairs extended past the back of the original house and formed a small enclosed addition with a corrugated tin roof. My older brother spent many hours sitting on that roof, which we could get to through my parents' bedroom window upstairs. We would also get sheets or other large pieces of cloth and parachute down off the roof into the backyard.

From the top of that roof, we could survey a slice of our neighborhood: the large breadfruit tree in the backyard of the Old London bar at the intersection of Irish Town Road and Fines Avenue, which seemed to tower over all the houses; the rooftop of our outdoor kitchen shed directly in front of us, and the tree growing out of the back of it, where birds came and went; Mrs. Allen's yard on the left-hand side; and Mrs. Gerald's yard on the right, which was shared by two other small houses.

Mrs. Allen was warm and friendly and a great cook. She took a special liking to Alfonso, one of my younger brothers, and would always fix him a plate of food, from which the rest of us managed to get a taste. Mrs. Gerald was also friendly, but her husband, Mr. Thomas, was a bit strange. Occasionally, we would wake up, along with our other neighbors late at night, to find Mr. Thomas on top of his roof yelling and talking incoherently. No one ever explained to me what caused Mr. Thomas to act this way, but the next day it would be over, and we would all go back to our routines, and Mr. Thomas would fade into the background of our lives, a quiet, distant, and unremarkable figure.

The second house in Mrs. Gerald's yard was old and deteriorating, and periodically occupied by a family whom we did not know very well. The third house was really more of a shack. An old woman lived there. We kids considered the woman to be both strange and ominous. She did not interact with others in the neighborhood, but went about her business, dressed strangely, talking to herself mysteriously, and in our ignorance, we feared and disliked her. We would sometimes toss pebbles at her from our living room window upstairs.

I never made the connection between the stoning that we experienced for what seemed like several months, and our throwing pebbles at our odd neighbor. The throwing of pebbles was a game, a malicious one, but not intended to inflict bodily harm, but the stoning was a terror, that could easily have resulted in death or serious injury.

There was a neighbor in the back of our house and to the left, directly behind Mrs. Allen's yard, across the narrow alley that ran behind our back fence. They were in fact exactly in line with the papau tree in Mrs. Allen's backyard; the tree whose sweet fruit we occasionally tasted. We never knew these people, but their house was raised up so that from their front door and porch, they looked down into our yard and those of our other neighbors. I thought they were the most likely suspects for the stoning. Stones the size of a man's fist would rain down on our backyard, several times a day, at unpredictable intervals. We were terrified, but cautiously went about our business, staying out of the backyard as much as possible.

I never learned the reason for the stoning. I am not sure how my parents dealt with it, but I don't recall seeing the police. It seems like it went on for months, but it may have been only weeks. Meanwhile, something else strange was going on. My friends at Irish Town School stopped speaking to and playing with me. And as we walked to church, the other kids shunned us. I don't remember anyone saying anything specific that would explain these strange happenings. I just lived in limbo and exile for the time it lasted. Then one day, inexplicably, my best friend at school started talking with me and playing with me again.

In retrospect, I understand that prior to these events, my mother and father separated. My father moved out and went to England, and my mother began seeing my stepfather, who was twelve years younger than she. I don't understand why this would so offend the morals of the community, since it was common for people there to have extramarital relationships, and men even occasionally were known to openly maintain two separate families. And in this case, my parents' stormy marriage had failed, and they had separated. I can only speculate that perhaps it was the fact that my mother was so much older than the man who would become my stepfather, and she had six children from two marriages. Perhaps the community felt that she was corrupting or taking advantage of an eligible and attractive young man. The irony is that my stepfather was already a playboy, as I myself saw one day when I took a message to him at his workshop, in the back of his mother's house.

In his workshop, he carved beautiful tombstones out of marble and granite. But in between, he apparently also played around with young women, one of whom I saw in the shop when I went to deliver the message. I never said anything to my mother, but as one of my childhood friends told me when we talked as adults, my stepfather was known to be a playboy. He was a puzzle, a man with very real talents, and who could also be very gentle. I remember him grinding carrots to make carrot juice for my baby brother, when my mother left us with him in St. Kitts for a year, while she came to the United States to earn money to bring us here. I also loved helping him as he carved beautiful praying hands onto a headstone as he worked at our house. Then I would also go with him to the cemetery to install the headstone. It was so peaceful, just the two of us working, among the green grass, graves, and flowers.

When he joined us in the U.S., he became a carpenter, first working for another man, and then starting his own business. But the partying and drinking with his buddies became more and more predominant. He deteriorated morally and physically over the years, becoming a serious alcoholic and a lecherous man. He died in his early fifties of an enlarged heart. I regret now that I refused to attend his funeral, because I was so angry at what he had done to my mother and our family. May God forgive him and me.

As individuals and as communities, we are caught in a dilemma when others offend our sense of what is morally acceptable. We feel that justice and the need for order and consequences require us to punish the offender. But the Christian admonishment that none of us is without sin should lead us to look deeper into our own hearts to see whether justice is truly the issue in a particular instance, or whether we are simply acting out of our own fear, hatred, and inability to forgive. And when justice does require punishment of an offense, we must punish while also forgiving, understanding that "all have sinned and fall short of the glory of God."[12]

Miss Baby Chases the Demon

"The demonic blinds; it does not reveal. In a state of demonic possession the mind is not really "besides itself," but rather it is in the power of elements of itself which aspire to be the whole mind which grasp the center of the rational self and destroy it. There is, however, a point of identity between ecstasy and possession. In both cases the ordinary subject-object structure of the mind is put out of action. But divine ecstasy does not violate the wholeness of the rational mind, while demonic possession weakens or destroys it."

— PAUL TILLICH[13]

We moved out of the house on Fines Avenue in Basseterre and

lived in a place called the Village for the period when I was three to eight years old. Miss Baby and her husband Houston lived next door. They had no children, so my brother Leroy and I commandeered their yard as a natural extension of our playground domain. Miss Baby's yard had some attractions that ours lacked. She had a star-apple tree in the front, with sweet fruit, the likes of which I have not tasted for more than forty years. In the back, she had a ginnip tree, which had sweet tangy fruit about the size of grapes, only more spherical, with one large seed in the middle, and a green skin thick enough to peel. The ginnip grew in bunches on a tree towering more than thirty feet high, with strong limbs and branches, that I might have tried to climb if I had been older and more daring.

Miss Baby's backyard also had a peppermint shrub, the smell of which was as attractive as its thorny branches were repellant. I don't know that Miss Baby's yard had any more interesting insects than did ours, though I do remember the scare we got when we saw my younger brother Tony, who was born when we were up in the Village, lying on his back on the ground playing with an eight-inch centipede on his bare stomach. Unlike Tony, I was old enough to know that centipedes can bite. His innocence protected him in this case, and he was not bitten.

Out on the street, we also found activities to maintain our interest that did not require our parents to spend money they did not have on toys. For instance, we raced small bits of wood we called boats in the storm drains that ran alongside the curbs, which seemed to have water even when it was not raining. The clear water seemed to run from the mountains down to the sea. At the intersection, it passed through a tunnel under the cross street and reappeared on the other side, which added an element of suspense to the boat race. One could be leading when the boats went into the tunnel and behind when they came out the other side, or vice versa.

We were only about three or four houses from the intersection, and if we turned right, the closest neighborhood store was on the immediate right. Facing the little store was a mysterious little circle, with a stone and brass object in the middle that looked like it may have been a large fountain in a former life. In my experience, there was never any water there, and nothing ever happened there to suggest the purpose of this circle. But the fountain-like object had carved green brass lions around it, facing in each direction like guardians. The road wound around the fountain and went down to the left toward Tanti's house; Tanti was my father's sister. To get to Tanti's though, we had to walk past the "crazy house" and the "poor house," which both sat far back from the road, with grasses and bushes between them and the road. We didn't understand much about these places, just that we were fortunate not to be in them ourselves, or to have any family members in them.

Miss Baby's house was identical to ours, made of concrete, and raised off the ground about three or four feet. The space underneath the house had a dirt floor and could be used for storing things. Willie lived underneath Miss Baby's house. He earned his living pulling heavy loads on a large manual wooden cart. The cart had steel wheels about six inches in diameter. It was the kind of wheel that we boys used to make wooden scooters or go-carts. Each wheel had a steel outer edge, rather than a rubber tire, and an inner steel hub through which we inserted the wooden axle. Between the steel hub and the outer steel rim, a set of steel ball bearings enabled a smooth almost friction-free motion, and created a characteristic singing, hissing sound against the paved street.

Willie's cart had a flat wooden bed, which sat perhaps a foot above the road. The front wheels were attached to a block of wood, like a two-by-four, which was attached to the rest of the cart by a short wooden neck. The wooden front axle could turn freely on the neck to change directions. Willie had a rope tied to both ends of sides of the axle, near each of the front wheels. He provided locomotion by either pulling the cart or by pushing from the rear. I believe he also had some sort of wooden braking system for slowing the cart going downhill. Willie would haul tremendous loads in his cart. I had seen him pulling and sweating, his feet bare.

On one occasion, my brother Leroy raided Willie's piggy bank, the can with coins that he kept underneath the house. I watched transfixed by a mixture of guilt and greed as he took out some of the silver coins. I don't remember if I got any of the money or anything bought with it, but I certainly did not report my brother's theft to our parents or other adults. I don't recall what became of Willie, but he seems to have disappeared from my consciousness after that incident. Miss Baby eventually went away to England as some people occasionally did in this former British colony. Other people would go away to America, or sometimes visit from America, like our cousin Hanna did.

While we were neighbors of Miss Baby, she and my mother often talked across the fence during breaks from their household chores, such as cooking and washing clothes by hand. Sometimes I eavesdropped on these conversations. The trick was to stay within earshot, but at a respectful distance. This distance was established, on one hand, by the free pursuit of my own interests in the play possibilities of the plants, animals, and inanimate objects is our yard, and, on the other, by my attraction to the sometimes fascinating things that the women discussed. I seldom had the chance to listen to my father and the neighboring men talk. They rarely stood still long enough around us children, except perhaps when occasionally playing dominoes, which did not seem conducive to interesting conversation.

But when the women talked, they were something to see. They didn't just use words. Using dramatic gestures, they would passionately act out little plays right before my eyes. Like the woman who ran a bakery where I used to go to pick up my family's daily bread each morning when I was about nine. She told a story one morning about a child who had gotten injured, perhaps by a fall. As she described how she picked up the child, she embraced a sheet of baked rolls and, holding it to her chest, touchingly acted out every gesture and word that she had communicated to the child. Everyone in the bakery seemed caught up in the emotion of her story.

That's the way it was when mother and Miss Baby were talking. I remember one particular conversation in which Miss Baby described being in her house one day when she became aware that a demonic spirit was present in the room with her. It was something like a calendar flapping on the wall that made her aware of this evil spirit. As she spoke, I experienced the fear she had experienced, but also her courage and determination to combat this demon, and to cast it out of her house. I don't remember what specific words she used to cast out the demon. It may have been in the name of God or Jesus Christ. But in strong words and gestures, she brought all that was good to bear in the life and death struggle against evil, one on one.

Forty-five years later, in a Baptist Church in Maryland, I experienced directly something related to what Miss Baby must have dealt with. She was alone, which was surely more terrifying, while I was in a large group at a Sunday morning church service. It's a given that in an African-American Baptist church service, there is an expectation of an almost tangible experience of the Holy Spirit—tears of joy and sadness, shouts of hallelujah and amen, hand clapping and dancing, and shouting and jumping around in a state seeming totally oblivious to the worshippers' physical surroundings. As we begin praise and worship at the start of the service, one can usually sense the spiritual temperature of the gathering. Almost without exception, every service reaches a degree of genuineness and spontaneity, where the words from the Scriptures, the music and lyrics of the gospel songs, and the rhythm and content of the sermon touch the hearts of the body of worshippers.

Some Sunday services are more Spirit-filled than others, but on this particular day, it felt as though there was some sort of invisible fog in the room, which muffled and swallowed up every attempt of the corporate body to establish a feeling of genuineness and sacredness. I felt the oppressiveness of it before anyone said anything about it. The usual order of services is for a team to lead the attendees in singing gospel songs and praising God for fifteen minutes before the pastor and other ministers enter the sanctuary.

On this morning, the pastor had been in the sanctuary for about thirty minutes when he stood and announced that there was a foul spirit in the place and that he could not sit still and let things continue as they were. He ordered that the doors of the church be opened and commanded, "In the name of Jesus," that the demonic spirit leave the building. The assembled body responded enthusiastically with clapping and shouts, and the atmosphere in the room changed. It became conducive to communicating with the Holy Spirit. The pastor explained to visitors that he was not condemning or driving out any person, only an evil spirit that may have come with a person.

In truth, I don't know whether or not Miss Baby's experience with her demon was similar to our experience in the Baptist church. I'm sure that her experience was terrifying, while mine was merely oppressive. I do not suggest that spiritual experiences are real in the scientifically observable sense. Rather, they are real in an experiential sense, in a manner that can transform an individual life as well as our collective history.

It was through the revelations of Abraham, Jesus, Mohammed, Buddha, and others, not just through scientific findings and philosophical discourse, that the higher values of humanity have become meaningful to most of the world's population. To seek to obtain and accumulate for oneself the most pleasure, power, and material wealth possible is the expected goal of humanity when viewed from the perspective of biological evolution. Revelation intervened in history to make spiritual goals real and worthy of the sacrifice of obvious self-interest.

The humanistic psychologist Abraham Maslow came to value more and more the importance of spiritual experience, what he called peak experiences. He divided humanity into two groups: peakers who value and have personal mystical experiences, and non-peakers "who have never had them or who repress or suppress them and who, therefore, cannot make use of them for their personal therapy, personal growth, or personal fulfillment."[14] He sought to find the common elements in mystical experiences, and thought that these were the essence, and that the cultural, historical, and other specific elements were unessential, and therefore could be discarded.

Today, one could go further than Maslow and say that mystical experiences are caused by the activation of certain parts of the brain in combination, and leave out all content. For example, physiological psychologist Michael Persinger has used systematic application of complex electromagnetic fields to induce mystical experiences involving sensing a presence that are perceived by his subjects as beings ranging from gods to aliens.[15] This complements the work of neurologist Andrew Newberg and his colleagues who have used brain scans to detect a common pattern of brain activity in meditating Buddhist monks and Catholic nuns.[16] So there are common elements to the subjective experience of mystical or spiritual experiences, and there are common physiological elements.

But it is the symbolic content of the mystical experience that makes it meaningful to people, and transformative for individual lives as well as for human history. Jesus and Mohammed both linked their revelations back through centuries of history and prophets back to Abraham. A messiah was predicted and expected by the Jewish prophets, but Jesus, a suffering Messiah dying on a cross, was "a stumbling block to the Jews . . ." because the reality he presented conflicted with their expectations.[17] Revelation is transformative, at least in part because it connects with history yet results in something new and unexpected.

I think Maslow was mistaken in his belief that we could abstract the common elements from mystical experiences and teach them devoid of the cultural, historical, and other specific elements. "Revelation, whether it is original or dependent, has revelatory power only for those who participate in it, who enter into the revelatory correlation."[18] By original revelations, Tillich means for Christians the revelation of Jesus experiencing himself as the Christ or Messiah, and being received as such by believers. Subsequent revelations within the Christian faith are dependent upon that original revelation. To experience either type of revelation, as opposed to acquiring knowledge through reasoning, requires that one experiences a relationship with God within one's own cultural and historical context, with connective roots back to the historical and cultural sources of the original revelation.

Physical Death, Spiritual Life

> *"The mind of sinful man is death, but the mind controlled by the Spirit is life and peace."*
>
> — ROMANS 8:6[19]

> *"For the ending of our life would not threaten us if we had not falsely made ourselves the centre of life's meaning. . . . The Christian answer is faith in the God who is revealed in Christ and from whose love neither life nor death can separate us."*
>
> — REINHOLD NIEBUHR[20]

Rags and the Hunter

Our dog Rags first introduced me to the reality of death. I must have been not much older than two years old, for it was before I started Mrs. Thompson's preschool at around the age of three. I was wandering about under our house on Fines Avenue in

Basseterre. At that time, the wooden house had no basement, so that I could extend the size my playground to include the yard and under the house. Rags was tied up at one corner of the house, and I kept my distance from him. But a little black-and-white kitten was not so wise, and ended up dying in Rags's jaws. I didn't actually see Rags do the deed, but I saw the kitten lying dead under the house and surmised that it was Rags's handiwork.

Rags was a large shaggy dog of undetermined breed, who seems to have come into existence before I did, and to have been tied up at the corner of the house for eternity. He was never allowed to run loose, apparently because he could not be relied upon not to bite people. Poor Rags. That may have been what led to his ultimate fate, early one morning, on the deserted beach, near the rocky ocean cliffs where the "boobies," or pelicans, roosted.

By the time of that fateful morning, we were living in the house in the Village, with the big yard and the calabash tree in the back. The calabash stood at the far end of the yard, near the outhouse and the fence. We could slip through the fence and pass into the alley, where men sitting at a table sometimes played dominoes. The calabash tree was itself a fascinating entity. Its fruit were big and round like cannonballs, and smelled really foul. But when you scraped out the soft smelly insides and dried out the shell, you could create a gourd that could be used to bail or drink water. The hummingbirds were also quite interested in the calabash tree. I would sit on a small concrete platform at the back of the yard, which looked like it was previously the floor of a small shed, and watch the hummingbirds flitting around the calabash tree.

Our backyard was also a highway of sorts for some large gray lizards, which scampered across it from the neighbor's yard to their homes under the concrete foundation of our outdoor kitchen. A portion of the foundation jutted out from the kitchen. There was a water pipe there, and the extended platform served as a place for washing and bathing. I remember the platform well; on the first day at Mrs. Thompson's preschool, I soiled my pants and was ignominiously walked the two miles or so to that platform and washed down. A guava tree grew behind the kitchen shed and extended its branches over the roof. From the guava fruit, my mother would periodically make guava jam, and a soft candy called guava cheese.

The house in the Village was made of concrete, with a concrete porch on the front. The living room door opened onto the porch. I remember sitting in the living room and hearing my father expressing his deep sense of being offended, because when he asked one of my older cousins if he wanted something to eat, my cousin answered, "If you can afford it." The concrete porch had stairs leading to a smaller front yard and the street. The front yard and the yard on the side of the house also had interesting small trees and flowers that attracted bees, all of which I viewed as part of my domain and playground. My friends and I also extended our playground to the yards and trees of the houses closest to mine.

Rags's abode was under the house as it had been on Fines Avenue. My father would also store planks and ladders and other things from his house painting business under the house as well. Those were not a problem for Rags. What would become Rags's problem could be found by going down the alley behind the house to a large open playing field. My father occasionally played a rough form of dodge ball with other men on the playing field. It was also the place where I and the other kids from Mr. Pete's school played during recess. Sometimes there was a horse tethered at the park. One day I went to touch the horse and woke up lying on the ground, stunned but otherwise unhurt.

The man who would be Rags's nemesis lived in the alley near the park. He was an object of some curiosity for me and the other children. Sometimes when we walked through the alley past his house, he would be sitting outside polishing his gun. He was known to be a hunter, and appeared to us to be a very heroic figure. Early one morning, my father took Rags and me for a walk, and we stopped at the hunter's house. The hunter then joined us in our walk. I had no idea where we were going and for what purpose, and to this day I don't quite understand why my father took me with them.

I really did not have a lot of direct contact or conversation with my father. I remember walking with him once to buy a pair of shoes, and he asked me about school. I know that it was important to him that I did well academically, because he and my mother sacrificed their meager resources to put my brother and me in private school. I also remember him scolding me once when I was doing something wrong, but for the most part, my mother administered the discipline of the children. He also took me once on a painting job with his crew. I helped them scrape old paint off the walls in a big old mansion that sat off the other side of the playing field. Beyond that, I knew him only as a stern and distant man who had a violent temper. That violence was directed at my mother, but not at the children.

That violent temper ultimately led to my parents separating, and to my father going away to England. At the time that they separated, we were back living at the house on Fines Avenue in Basseterre. After he moved out, my father came back once when we were home from school for lunch period. He ended up arguing with my mother, taking our radio (a prized possession), and breaking in on the ground, while the neighbors gathered around and watched. A year or so later, when I was ten years old, we heard that he had been killed in England. He and another sign painter had been struck by a train as they worked on the railroad tracks. I regret to say that when I heard this, my immediate feeling was one of relief. Later, trains haunted my dreams for many years as a young man.

But on this morning, I was just happy to be out for a walk with my father, the hunter, and our dog Rags. Rags was also happy. It was so rare that he got the chance to run around freely. He bounded from one interesting spot to another, as we made our way. We went down the hill past the playing field, and headed toward the ocean. This was an isolated beach, not one to which we usually went. When we were in that general area, we usually walked on the road that wound around the bend of the island over the rock cliffs where the "boobies" swooped and cried. But today we headed down onto the beach.

The beach was apparently used by someone, because there was a small fishing boat pulled up onto the sand. I still didn't understand what was going on, but my father or the hunter told me to go and sit behind the boat while they took Rags to the other side. Shortly, there was a loud bang, and I came out from behind the boat. Rags lay in the sand dead, and covered with blood. I was in shock. My father and the hunter dug a grave in the sand and buried Rags as I watched. I don't remember the walk home.

Angela's Train

When my family emigrated to the United States in 1962, we first lived on South Seventh Avenue in Mount Vernon, New York, with my Uncle Walford, his wife Auntie Ann, and their children. I still don't understand how six of them and seven of us all fitted into the two floors of that house, but we did, until Uncle Walford and his family bought another house and moved out. Angela lived next door. She was a few years younger than I, so we really didn't have a direct relationship. She was one of the children in the neighborhood, and she did similar things to what the rest of us did. So what happened to her could have happened to any of us.

Our houses and the neighborhood wrapped us in a warm security blanket, that for me was punctured periodically by a run-in with a bully, who didn't like my West Indian accent; or by the wise guy who would pick the lock on my bike parked at a store, and watch and laugh when I returned and found it unlocked. He didn't want to steal my bike. He just enjoyed letting me know that he could steal it anytime he wanted to.

I was twelve years old, and proud of my bike, because I had bought it myself, with money earned from my paper route. I was a kid from a tiny Caribbean island who had never seen snow except on a Christmas card. Now I was trudging through the snow delivering newspapers several blocks from my house. I was such an alien that ambulances appeared to me as strikingly strange vehicles. I also thought that a man on my paper route, whose face was red from the cold, might be one of those "red men" I had heard about, who populated North America before the Europeans arrived. This was truly a different world that my family and I had to adjust to. When we first arrived at the airport, it was nineteen degrees Fahrenheit, so our uncle had brought some coats for us to put on as we came out of the airplane. My seven-year-old brother, who had never experienced temperatures colder than about seventy degrees, exclaimed, "Take this coat off me; it's making me cold."

Our immediate neighborhood consisted mostly of African-American families, with a small number of older white people, but no white children. A few blocks to the south, it became mostly white. At Washington Junior High, four blocks from my house, the student body was a mix of whites and African-Americans. I had come from a place where there were few white people. In St. Kitts, my stepfather did have a white drinking buddy, who occasionally came to pick him up. And in my last year in St. Kitts, I attended the Grammar School, where I became friendly with one white boy. He and his mother would sometimes give me a ride home when she came to pick him up. In Mount Vernon, I was not aware of race as an issue, or of the civil rights movement and all the changes that were occurring around the country. I saw a poster of Elijah Mohammed of the Nation of Islam on a utility pole next to my house, but it meant nothing to me, and I never heard anyone discussing it.

My friends were black, except for a stocky, slightly chubby, white boy from my school named Johnny. Johnny lived several blocks from me, in the opposite direction from Washington Junior High, and I would sometimes walk to his house to play with him and his friends. I remember once we inspected the stump of a giant tree that had been cut down in his backyard, trying to figure out how old it was by the number of rings.

Eventually, the kids who I became closest to were the twins, Donald and Ronald, who were in some of my classes. I was especially close to Donald, and he and I took swimming lessens at the YMCA. The twins, some other boys, and I formed a group based on our common interest in racing toy slot cars, listening to rhythm-and-blues music on transistor radios, and riding our bikes on long exploratory day trips. Sometimes these trips took us to the ocean, where we fished off the rocks or pier. My friends always seemed to know where they were going. I had no idea, but felt perfectly secure in their company.

But before I met Donald and Ronald, I spent time with another set of twins who lived on my block. One of the things the kids on my block did during the summer was to walk to Wilson Pool to go swimming. To get to and from the pool, we frequently walked along the railroad tracks. That was an important part of the trip because we would sometimes find ripe blackberries growing along the track, which we would pick and eat as we went along.

Angela and her friends apparently did the same thing, because one day we heard that there had been a train accident, and that Angela was killed walking on the tracks. The kids on the block were stunned that one of us, who had been playing around the street and yards so recently, was gone. I, and some of the other children, attended the church service. Angela was really gone. And though I was not personally close to her, I felt that a part of us was gone forever.

My father had been killed by a train when I was ten years old.

But that occurred in England, while we were still in St. Kitts. He and my mother had also been separated for some time. In addition, at the time of his death, my most vivid recent memory of my father was of him coming to my mother's house and smashing our radio in a fit of rage. So his death did not affect me at that time as a personal emotional loss. I also did not see his body or attend his funeral service because he was buried in England. I had viewed the body of my stepfather's brother, who had died about a year after my father died, while we were still in St. Kitts. But I had never met this step-uncle when he was alive. So I viewed his body, after it was prepared for burial, with a somewhat detached, and almost scientific curiosity. I noticed, for example, that he had a fresh small cut on his chin or jaw, possibly from being shaved after death.

Angela's death was the first one that I experienced at a direct personal and emotional level. Angela was a real living child like me, and now she was gone. After her death, we no longer walked along the railroad tracks and picked blackberries.

My Mother's Death

One day in 1989 I got a disturbing phone call from my mother in which she was confused and clearly not herself. She was about seventy years old, and lived by herself in an apartment in a public housing project in a lower middle class section of the Bronx. The apartment was about fifteen minutes from the duplex brick house that she previously owned in a similar neighborhood on Laconia Avenue. That brick house was the last one I had lived in with my family before leaving for college. The neat brick houses, with their hedges out front, had shared driveways separating each duplex, leading to a duplex garage, and separate little backyards. In the backyard, which was covered with concrete and enclosed by a wire fence and the garage, I had constructed a dog house for Dingo.

Moving from the house we rented from Uncle Walford in Mount Vernon, New York, to a house of our own, just across the boundary in New York City, disruptive my life at the age of fifteen. Having finally settled into my Mount Vernon neighborhood after moving thousands of miles from St. Kitts, it was traumatic to leave Donald and Ronald and our little group of friends. Leaving Mount Vernon High School in the middle of the tenth grade was also difficult. This was the year when everything began coming together for me academically. I had been improving as I became acclimated to the U.S. school system through seventh, eighth, and ninth grades. Now, at the beginning of the tenth grade, without any special effort on my part, I knew all the answers and was the best student in each of my classes. Biology, geometry, social studies, and all the other subjects seemed open, obvious, and inviting. Teachers noticed and gave me positive attention.

My social studies teacher, Ms. Kass, in particular, seemed to take a special interest in me. On the outside, she was a bright, sharp-tongued, sarcastic, and pretty young woman, who obviously knew a lot more than she was able to teach us. She was intimidating in class. But she had a motherly side as well. She would give me extra books to read, such as Voltaire, and encourage me to think well beyond the bounds of tenth grade social studies. It was during one of her classes that the Mount Vernon school administration caught up with me, having discovered that I had moved recently out of Mount Vernon and no longer belonged in its school system.

I was called to the front office and interrogated. I quickly broke down and cried. Ms. Kass came by the office, sharply told me to stop crying, and promised to do whatever she could to help me. Alas, there was nothing she could do about jurisdictional boundaries and bureaucracies, so with a broken heart, I was transferred to Evander Childs High School in the Bronx. But God was merciful, and I again found teachers who nurtured me, captivated by the combination of my intellectual ability and social ineptness.

That move to Laconia Avenue was at a time of optimistic economic upward mobility for my mother and stepfather. My stepfather had transferred his tombstone carving skills to carpentry, at which he was clearly talented. For a while, he worked for a white man in Mount Vernon who had his own carpentry business. I never saw the man do any manual work, and or saw any other workers, but he seemed to know carpentry, and my stepfather seemed to learn a lot from him. After we were at Laconia Avenue for a year or so, my stepfather left his employer and started his own carpentry business.

Things seemed to be going so well, but the seeds of eventual dissolution were already budding. My stepfather's drinking and socializing with his group of loud buddies, for whom he would cook special dinners of shrimp or steak, continued to escalate. And the womanizing also continued. I missed the worst part of it by going off to college. Eventually they lost everything: the house on Laconia as well as another house in Mount Vernon that my mother's cousin, whom we called Uncle Joe, had left her. My mother had taken care of Uncle Joe when he was sick and dying, and he had willed her his house. But my stepfather's drinking destroyed their finances, and he left her in the ruins and went back to St. Kitts.

My mother's next move continues to confound me, and revealed her most profound weakness. She sold both houses, moved with the four remaining children into an apartment in the same general area, and used the money to finance a trip back to St. Kitts to find and bring back my stepfather. I was at home for a visit on the day Mother left for St. Kitts. Uncle Walford drove her to the airport, and I particularly enjoyed listening to him talk during the drive about his adventures as a jazz band leader, traveling around the Caribbean. He was a good storyteller and had a confident and optimistic view of his life. He talked about giving up music and becoming a welder, when he met Auntie Ann and settled down. I admired him a lot, and was a little envious of the stable family life he and Auntie had provided for my cousins, compared to the three unhappy marriages that my mother had had.

But, as I said when I eulogized her when she died at age seventy-nine, my mother was my hero. "To the world, she was an ordinary, hardworking mother, who worked in jobs at the lower end of the social ladder, in order to make a life for her children and herself. But I am amazed at the determination, love, and sacrifice she showed in moving herself and her then six children from the small island of St. Kitts in the Caribbean, to the outskirts of New York City, one of the largest and most complex cities on earth . . . like a hero in the classical tradition, mother had tremendous strengths, but she also had a striking weakness . . . her weakness was in choosing men who were far more flawed than she."

My mother did manage to bring my stepfather back to the United States. And their economic decline continued. At the bottom, I visited them when they were living in an apartment in the South Bronx with my three younger brothers and younger sister. We had certainly known poverty in St. Kitts, but not accompanied by the kind of physical and social alienation that this neighborhood projected. This new physical environment was alien to anything we had previously experienced. In walking from the subway to the apartment, I had the impression of a type of war zone, with canyons of old, decaying, and downright ugly buildings. The building they lived in was depressingly consistent with the neighborhood. They were at the end of the road, and a conversation I had with my stepfather confirmed my impression of the neighborhood. Appalled at the situation they were in, I confronted him saying that he had to make a choice between his family and his alcohol. In a shocking display of honesty, he responded angrily, "If I have to make that choice, then my choice will be alcohol."

They did not stay there long. Soon my mother faced the reality that holding on to my stepfather would mean continued pain and destruction for herself and her children. It was only many years later that I learned what my sisters and younger brothers had had to endure, beginning back at the brick duplex on Laconia Avenue. My stepfather's drinking and womanizing had been present from the first time he came into our lives in St. Kitts. But there was also the dedicated craftsman who carved praying hands on tombstones, and the caring stepfather who grated carrots to make juice for my youngest brother, and who took care of us, while my mother went away to the United States for a year, in order to make enough money to come back and get us. In him, a battle between good and evil had surely been waged, and evil won.

After he separated from my mother, my stepfather did eventually stop drinking because he had an enlarged heart, and the doctors told him he would die if he continued to drink. I don't know whether he relapsed into drinking again, or whether the physical damage was already fatal. But he died from that enlarged heart.

My mother did manage to move out of the South Bronx within a few months and into an apartment in the public housing complex close to her former house. That was the apartment from which she called me that day, confused and alone. My youngest brother lived not far from her and was the one who looked after her. It seemed a mutually agreeable arrangement; he got some home cooking and his laundry done. Mother had a controllable form of heart disease, for which she was prescribed nitroglycerin paste. She rubbed the paste on her chest when she had chest pains. She had also had a recent incident in which she had had to be hospitalized briefly, for what appeared to be a seizure or mild stroke. The doctors discovered that she had a benign but inoperable tumor in her brain, which may have been the cause of the incident requiring her hospitalization.

She appeared to have recovered after the brief hospital stay and was back to being herself at home. But now, the strange phone call, in which she was talking and laughing in a way that did not make sense, clearly indicated that she was not well. After conferring with my youngest brother, the caretaker, and my sisters in Atlanta,

I decided to go to New York (from Boston) and try to help. When I arrived at my mother's apartment, it broke my heart to see her mental state. She was incoherent and kept obsessing about a little box, in which she kept an insurance policy and other documents that were important to her. I felt pained because I could see that she knew in some way that something was wrong, that she may be dying, and wanted to take care of her business so as not to be a burden on her children. That was my interpretation at least, and it was consistent with what I knew of her.

My bother and I called the ambulance and rode with her to the hospital. By the time we got there, she was having a massive seizure, and we feared for the worst. We sat in the cold uncomfortable waiting room all night, expecting that this might be the end. By morning, nothing had been clarified, and mother was alive but still incoherent. For several days, we went back and forth, from the apartment to the hospital, waiting for them to find a bed for her. Meanwhile, she was in the crowded emergency room. The scene reminded me of the New York subways at rush hour. Beds were lined up in the emergency room and patients lay there for days waiting for an inpatient bed to become available. Having by now spent most of my life in Boston, with several advanced medical centers within a small area, I was horrified to see the state of care at a medical center in New York City.

Eventually, my mother did get a bed on one of the hospital wards. When I visited her there, she was still incoherent. I don't remember if she appeared to recognize us, but she definitely could not communicate with us. It seemed like weeks went by without any change, and the doctors told us that she would be moved to a rehabilitation center, but that they were doubtful that she would recover her speech and other intellectual functions.

Mother spent several months in the rehabilitation center, and eventually did recover her speech, her sense of humor, and the ability to walk about briskly. My wife Glenda, my daughter

Darrilyn, and I visited her at the center. By then she had begun forming relationships with some of the staff and other patients and seemed generally happy. She wondered aloud that God must have spared her for a purpose, but she didn't know what. She became tearful at times, and was worried about what would become of her once she left the center.

After that visit, Glenda, who had recently lost her own mother to cancer, suggested that we move my mother to Boston to live with us. Soon after that, I drove back to New York, packed up my mother's things from her apartment, and she and I drove to Boston. My brothers and sisters and I shared the expense of hiring someone to stay at our house with Mother during the day. Despite our best intentions, having Mother living with us in our small house in the Hyde Park section of Boston did not work for long. My mother was not totally the person I remembered. She now seemed to relate in strange ways to our fifteen-year-old daughter who was going through a difficult adolescence. At times mother would collude with Darrilyn and encourage her in intrigues with boyfriends, then at other times, she would accuse her of doing things that she was not supposed to. In addition to this, our twenty-two-year-old son Lorenzo was bouncing between our house and his grandmother's, having dropped out of high school in the tenth grade and being able to remain employed only periodically in minimum wage service jobs.

My relationship with Glenda was at its lowest point. She displayed moodiness and temper, to the point where communication between us was becoming limited. In retrospect, I believe she was still depressed about her mother's death, which aggravated her normal tendency to be somewhat temperamental. I was focused on building a business, which absorbed a lot of my mental and emotional energies. And the situation no doubt exaggerated my natural tendency to be somewhat withdrawn and internally focused. The fabric of our family seemed to be disintegrating. The lowest point of this crisis period was when Darrilyn ran away from home for several days. If ever I needed God in my life and our lives, it was then. But at that point I was operating totally in the material world. Glenda and Darrilyn went to church, but that was not an activity that seemed relevant to me at that time. We spent a lot of time in psychotherapy in those years, mostly focused on the problems of our children.

Eventually, in an attempt to bring some order to the chaos of our household, we moved my mother, who had improved significantly in her ability to care for herself, to a studio apartment nearby. With this new configuration, and with continuing psychotherapy, we reached a level of functionality, which enabled Darrilyn to graduate from high school, Glenda to complete bachelor and master's degrees in education, and me to sustain a business that kept us afloat financially. Mother seemed to enjoy having her own space, with support and regular visits from us, and some home care assistance. When we moved to the adjacent town of Milton, we moved her to an apartment in an elderly housing building nearby.

I could not have the conversations that I enjoyed with Mother prior to her illness—when she would talk about her experiences and people she knew before I could remember. Because both sets of my grandparents died before I was born, my mother was the last tentative link with my past. Now her memory was poor, so we could only talk about the present and recent past. But she still had her sense of humor and that spark, as when she would smile knowingly, look at us with a mischievous twinkle in her eye, and boast, "The old lady is still shaking." Because of her brain tumor, her aging was not the typical one, where recent memory becomes dim and long-term memory is vivid. But thank God, it was also not like the illnesses of my Uncle Walford or Cousin Hanna, whose Alzheimer's disease totally obliterated their ability to recognize and relate to family members.

I am grateful that I got to spend the last eight years of my mother's life with her. I regret that I was not always as patient in responding to her needs as I should have been. I treasure the deep and cleansing grief I experienced at her loss, because that assured me that she and I were (are) connected. Everything that I value in myself is connected to her, and to that emotional and spiritual bond. This includes an apprehension of the Holy Spirit of God that cannot be explained away, and that causes me to weep with joy during a sermon or a gospel song. It lets me know that I am a child of God, in a way that is deeply rooted, and can never be intellectualized. And it's not just a passing emotionalism, or catharsis, because the tears water seeds that grow and bloom and enter more and more aspects of my everyday life, until nothing is more important than the experience of being with the Holy Spirit. My old self falls away, and I am a new person. My salvation is by the grace of God, but it is through my mother that I came to experience that grace.

I also thank her for music. She loved to sing. As a child following her around the house, I learned the emotional meaning of haunting songs of love and loss, such as "Tennessee Waltz." I did not learn to play music until my late teens, when I dropped out of college, and started beating on a set of bongo drums and playing a homemade flute. I did eventually return to college and studied flute and composition at Berklee College of Music, instead of returning to Harvard University. I would never be more than an amateur musician, but music has brought such depth to my life experience, that I would be impoverished without it.

Although she was not educated past high school, Mother loved to read and she wrote in a beautiful hand. She taught me to read and write, to love learning and to value education. Sometimes I have loved learning too much, for its own sake, beyond and against material gain, and sometimes, regretfully, before the love of God. My abuse of this gift is to my own discredit, for that she did not teach me.

I did not inherit or learn my mother's love and enjoyment of being with people. With her, it appeared to be natural and unpracticed. She liked people, and people liked her. With me, it is a skill that I have learned with great difficulty and not well. This is all the more reason why being with her in her last years and months of life was so essential for my own humanity.

And I almost cheated myself out of that experience. After Mother had been with Glenda and me for five years, it became necessary for business reasons to move to a Maryland suburb near Washington DC. For the two years before our move to Maryland, I commuted weekly from Boston. The responsibilities of care for my mother fell totally on Glenda's shoulders. I am forever grateful that Glenda treated her like her own mother, and they became close.

I was also expecting that I would be doing more traveling for business once we moved and thought that this might be the time to move Mother to Atlanta, where my two sisters, youngest brother, and their families lived. This did not work out, because my mother's relationships with my sisters were complicated by their feelings that she had let them down at critical points in their lives because of her desire to hold onto my stepfather, which was in fact the case.

So Glenda and I agreed to move Mother to Maryland with us. This also happened at the point where Mother was hospitalized, and it became clear that she could no longer live in her own apartment. We had an in-law apartment designed in the house that we built in Maryland, but by the time of our move, it was clear that she could not stay in the house without supervision. She would become socially isolated, relative to her previous situation of having an apartment in an elderly housing building. With the assistance of two good friends, a psychologist, and a psychiatrist in geriatrics, Mother was moved from the hospital to a rehabilitation facility in Boston, making it easier to transfer her to a nursing home in Maryland at the time of our move.

Nursing homes are now essential institutions for the way our lives are structured today. But institutional living, no matter how well managed, is an assault on the sensibilities of people who are used to running their own lives and managing their own personal space. Mother quickly made friends at the nursing home, particularly among the staff, many of whom were women from the Caribbean. Mother was mobile and able to function with minimal assistance within the structure of the facility, which in addition to her friendly personality, was a reason that the staff liked her. Her only obvious problem was that she could easily become disoriented, and it took her a while to learn her way around the halls, between her room and the dining room and other public areas.

The nursing home had a pretty backyard with trees and flowers, and Mother would sit on the back porch and smoke cigarettes with the other smokers. She had several roommates during the three years she lived there, and at least one of them disrupted her sleep by making noises or moving around at night. There was also a continuous problem with her clothes and other belongings. Her things were frequently missing, though all her clothes were marked. There was also a problem with keeping her clothes clean. She could not distinguish clean from dirty clothes and would hang her dirty clothes in the closet, mixed in with her clean clothes. She resisted the idea that she needed help with such basic self-care and gave the staff a hard time when we insisted that they help her to dress. The role reversal felt odd when I had to sit her down and insist that she let the staff help her get dressed. Despite these problems, she seemed happy there, and frequently joked with the staff. So though we felt some ambivalence and guilt about her living in an institution, we felt overall that she was at home there.

When we took her to our house overnight, she would become disoriented, so after a while we would bring her home only for the day and return her to the nursing home to sleep. So this became the pattern for three years. She was on a regimen of Dilantin for seizure prevention, and Cardizem for angina and high blood pressure. Her brain tumor remained stable, as did the resulting problems with memory and orientation. Once or twice her Dilantin level became too high, and she became paranoid and irrational until it was fixed. Ultimately, it was the Dilantin that precipitated the series of events that led to her death.

It began when she became toxic from the Dilantin and had to be hospitalized for several days. The Dilantin level was finally brought down, and she became rational again and could talk with us. She was discharged from the hospital back to the nursing home, but she was not able to get out of bed. Apparently she had contracted pneumonia from being in bed for about a week, and had to be rehospitalized. The doctors told us that we should be prepared for the worst, because a seventy-nine-year-old person would having difficulty surviving the stress that her body had experienced in two short weeks. They could help her to breathe and give her intravenous fluids and medication, but it was mostly up to her body to heal itself. She lay thrashing restlessly in the emergency room bed, and could not speak much, so they admitted her to intensive care.

The first day we saw her in intensive care, Mother was unconscious and was breathing with the help of a machine. She was in a small room with a window, directly across form the nursing station. My sisters and brothers and I had discussed it and agreed that we would not authorize extreme measures to try to keep her alive, but rather would let her die as peacefully as possible. The next evening when Glenda and I visited her she was conscious and alert, but still needed the machine to help her breathe. She said, as she often did, "Don't worry; Mother will be all right." I felt so happy at the apparent improvement in her condition. I really believed that she was going to get better. We did not want to tire her, so we did not stay long. If I had known that that was the last time I would see her alive, I would have said so much more. I would have told her how much I loved her, and that I admired her for what she had accomplished for us through years of toil and struggle.

The next morning, we got a call from her nurse saying that we should come in because, my mother would not last for much longer. I quickly dressed and left for the hospital. But as I came to the intersection where our street meets the main road, the nurse called me on my cell phone to let me know that mother had just died. She died peacefully and did not regain consciousness. When I got to the intensive care unit, her body was still warm. I stood in shock as the nurse told me that a chaplain would be coming soon, that I needed to make arrangements for a funeral home, and that if any other relatives were coming, they needed to come soon because they could not keep her body in an intensive care bed for long. The chaplain arrived and said something to me. Then he handed me a card with the twenty-third psalm printed on it, and began to recite it. As he read it, I was engulfed by a deep sweet sorrow, and my tears came in a seemingly endless stream. The sorrow was sweet because it reassured me that even though my mother was gone, she would forever be part of me. That sorrow connected me to her, and I was grateful for it. Because I knew that if I did not have the sorrow, it would be as if she were not real, our relationship was not real, and therefore I am not real. I would just be a bunch of thoughts, ideas, and impulses floating around in the ether. I cherished that sorrow then, and I still do as I write this today.

Soon Glenda came into the room and took care of everything that needed to be done. And that is how we operated for the next few days until the funeral. She made all the arrangements, and I did a lot of crying. All of my brothers and sisters and their families were staying at my house, except for my older brother Leroy who had died five years earlier in St. Kitts. Our daughter and granddaughter had also come down from Boston, and Auntie Ann and our cousins came on the day of the funeral. Uncle Walford had died the previous year.

My sisters, brothers, our spouses, and I discussed the finances and the program for the funeral. We agreed on who would take responsibility for what. As the oldest, I was asked to say something about Mother from the perspective of the family. I took this as an opportunity to recognize our mother's heroic struggle to bring her children from St. Kitts to a land of opportunity, and that our achievements are confirmation of her vision and courage. I also addressed her tragic flaw, her selection of husbands, one of whom was a wife beater, and the other an alcoholic and womanizer. After the funeral service, I was gratified that my brothers and stepbrother expressed that they felt that I had spoken for them.

The difficult part for me was not the sorrow and tears that I experienced immediately after my mother's death. Those were sweet, as I previously explained. But in the weeks following her burial, a dense opaque despair settled upon me, that was unambiguously painful. It felt as though all the systems in my body and mind were shutting down, as though I too was dying. I continued to walk through my daily routine, but with leaden steps, and without hope. Then slowly, the cloud receded, and life again became worth living.

I Will Fear No evil

> "*Even though I walk through the valley of the shadow of death,*
> *I will fear no evil, for you are with me; your rod and your staff,*
> *they comfort me.*"
>
> — PSALM 23:4[21]

> "*The four categories [time, space, causality, and substance] are*
> *four aspects of finitude in its positive and negative elements.*
> *They articulate the union of being and nonbeing in everything*
> *finite. They articulate the courage which accepts the anxiety of*
> *nonbeing. The question of God is the question of the possibility of*
> *this courage.*"
>
> — PAUL TILLICH[22]

On April 4, 2001, the day I was diagnosed with prostate cancer, I was in the middle of an effort to buy a business. The business operated employee assistance programs, providing counseling and referral services to employees. That day the bank told me that I would not only have to mortgage our house, but to personally provide a 20 percent equity down-payment before it would further consider the loan, even with a Small Business Administration guarantee. Given my diagnosis, I decided it was best not to be struggling under a large debt and increased stress. I now know that my frenetic business activities of that period were not just about business, but were my attempts to find ultimate satisfaction in something that is finite. "In true faith the ultimate concern is a concern about the truly ultimate; while in idolatrous faith preliminary, finite realities are elevated to the rank of ultimacy. . . . The inescapable consequence of idolatrous faith is 'existential disappointment', a disappointment which penetrates into the very existence of man!"[23]

I have at times envied people who from a young age knew exactly what they wanted to do with their lives, and efficiently spent their years focused on accomplishing that one set of goals. Unlike those people, I have been at times interested in several different things and, at others times, interested in nothing. I started college with a major in English because I enjoyed reading and writing, but I also simultaneously harbored the idea of becoming an electronics engineer. I liked to tinker and build things, and had blown the fuses in my parents' house at least once during one of my electronic kit experiments. But I ended up dropping out of college, experimenting with music, and working at a psychiatric hospital. When I did go back to college, I majored in music, but ended up going to graduate school in psychology. As soon as I finished my doctorate in psychology, I went to business school.

I have made a living for fifteen years managing two organizations that I cofounded that operate mental health and consulting services, so there is some retrospective logic to the combination of psychology and business. But within my business activities, I have experienced that same restlessness and dissatisfaction that is obvious in my young adulthood.

Being diagnosed with prostate cancer pulled me out of that cycle of endless striving and dissatisfaction, and focused my attention on the ultimate issues of life and death, finiteness and eternity. Or at least the striving became a faint noise in the background, relative to the issues of here and now. It was a reversal of the figure and ground, in terms of my focus prior to diagnosis. Before, I was engaged in daily spiritual practice, specifically reading the Bible every day. At that time, I was particularly interested in how the gospel was spread by the disciples after the departure of Jesus. So I was reading the New Testament from the Acts through Revelation. But my spiritual life was still a background to my business strivings. After my diagnosis, my spiritual life became the figure, and my business life the background.

Instead of rushing toward an anticipated future based on my efforts to realize my ambitions, I was forced to acknowledge that the future was beyond my control, and that I may not in fact have a future at all. I began to live more in the present, and to trust God and accept whatever future, life or death, I would face. Instead of fear and anxiety, I began to feel more frequently a sense of peace and optimism, even when the doctor's reports at times included some negative surprises.

Before the diagnosis, I did experience anxiety and apprehension on the day that I had a biopsy and scan performed at the hospital. The department where these procedures were performed was particularly disorganized in terms of the scheduling of patients, and the receptionist would disappear for long periods of time. I eventually had to grab a nurse or technician passing by to get myself into the proper queue for service. This is after I had spent more than an hour drinking a quart of an awful tasting pink creamy chemical milkshake that served as contrast agent for the scan. Another part of my discomfort may have been the nature of the biopsy. They did not take one sample from my prostate. Rather, they sampled fourteen different areas of the prostate using a kind of punching machine that make a terrible racket, like the snap of a giant electric stapler with each punch; and each one of them hurt. However, it did help that the doctor performing the biopsies was reassuring, and explained what he intended to do before he did it.

The scan was not a difficult procedure, but it did lead to some concerning results. Apparently my urologist was not aware that I had had Paget's disease, which changed the bone density in a part of my hip. When they saw this on the scan, they thought it was linked to the prostate cancer and immediately ordered x-rays of my hip to clarify the situation. I could tell by her tone when the nurse called me with the order for x-rays that they were concerned that my cancer may have spread to the bone. I told them about the Paiget's disease, and I did not worry about it. I felt confident that that was the cause of the bone density differences. That problem had already been treated and had been stable for five years.

Two weeks after my initial diagnosis of prostate cancer, my wife Glenda and I met with the urologist to discuss my test results. The good news was that the cancer was in the early stage and limited to the prostate. It was curable but would require a serious procedure, either surgery or radiation. It would require me to be out of the office for about one month. We would start the process the following week with a second opinion examination that my urologist had arranged. My urologist specialized in surgical procedures, while the second doctor specialized in treatments using radiation. My urologist's opinion was that surgery was the best treatment for my specific type of prostate cancer, but he wanted me to see someone who specialized in radiation treatment, so that I could be independently convinced of the best treatment option.

After the visit with my doctor, I felt a deep sense of gratitude for all the blessings in my life. I felt blessed that my cancer was treatable. I felt blessed that our daughter had recently come home with our two granddaughters after six years in a bad relationship. I felt blessed that our son was also home, was working, and was more stable than ever before.

But even while a part of me had stopped to smell the roses, another part continued to pursue business interests that would eventually turn out to be a waste of time and money. It would take me a full year after my prostate cancer treatment to realize and implement a permanent change in my activities. Meanwhile, I lived as if in two worlds, one where time had slowed to a crawl and everything was focused on the present, and the other, where I continued to run to catch something that felt essential to my existence. I began to think about training my staff to cover some of my duties while I was having treatment. Part of the problem with some of the business activities I was pursuing, was that they took a lot of my time, and kept me chained to other people's schedules. This was the opposite of what I really needed, but I did not know that then.

A week later, Glenda and I met with the doctor for a second opinion on my treatment of prostate cancer. He reiterated that it was an early stage cancer, and not aggressive, but should be treated because I am relatively young (age fifty) for this disease. I learned that prostate cancer becomes increasingly common as men get older, but most people die with it, rather than from it, because the progression of the disease is usually slow. If I were older, "watchful waiting" or doing nothing would be a viable treatment option. For me, the options were surgery to remove the prostate, external radiation, or implantation of radiation seeds.

While my life was no longer in apparent jeopardy, there were serious risks from any of the three procedures including: impotence, incontinence, and damage to the bladder, rectum, or other surrounding tissue. Surgery would involve hospitalization of up to one week, at-home recovery for three or four weeks, and up to a one-year healing period. Radiation seeds have a similar time frame, though the hospitalization and at-home recovery are shorter. External radiation requires eight weeks of daily twenty-minute treatments.

According to both my regular urologist and the consulting doctor, surgery was the most recommended treatment for my age and type of cancer, but either radiation therapies were also reasonable options. I was leaning strongly toward surgery. In discussing it further with Glenda, we agreed that it made sense to seek a third opinion. We thought Howard University Hospital would be a good source because of its experience with African-American men. News reports had followed Louis Farrakan's treatment at Howard the previous year for prostate cancer. So I made an appointment for the following Monday with the chief of urology at Howard. When Glenda and I saw him, he confirmed the diagnosis of early stage nonaggressive cancer that has a more than 90 percent likelihood of a total cure with surgery. He also commented that my urologist is well respected, having written one of the key articles in the field. This settled my mind, and now it became just a matter of scheduling the surgery so that it would be less likely to interfere with my business activities.

It was now early May, and my surgery was scheduled for June 6. This time of year, we are hit with the triple whammy of Mother's Day and the anniversaries of the deaths of my mother and my wife's mother all happening around the same time. Over one twenty-four-hour period, I experienced the most intense depressed moods and emotional volatility. I was preparing for major surgery, struggling to get a new business off the ground, and dealing with the joys and challenges of a household including adult children and grandchildren. But I think it was the triple whammy that really got me. I remembered that immediately after my mother's death two years earlier, the feeling of sorrow and the overwhelming tears actually felt cleansing and positive. The real difficulty came later with a period of intense and volatile moods, and the sometimes overwhelming feeling of despair. Those same moods that recurred last year now appeared again. I thanked God they don't last long anymore.

My surgery date arrived. Glenda was with me as I was prepped for surgery. I felt relaxed and confident. I slipped from consciousness comfortably, and next vaguely remember Glenda and my doctor saying something reassuring to me while I was in the recovery room. Later, in my hospital bed, they told me that my procedure had gone well, though some additional cancer was found in a lymph node outside the prostate. After this discovery at the beginning of the operation, my doctor had talked with Glenda about whether to proceed with the surgery. Fortunately, they decided to go ahead. My doctor thought that he had gotten all the cancer cells, but we would have to wait for the pathologist's report. Again I felt confident rather than worried. When it arrived, the final pathologist report showed that the cancer was intact within the prostate except for one small area. Similarly, the problematic lymph node was near the prostate and its cancer cells were also contained. Given the findings, my doctor thought it likely that we were successful in getting everything. In any case, this situation called for monitoring my prostate specific antigen (PSA) levels, and only initiating additional treatment if an elevated level was detected.

It had been about twenty years since I had stayed in a hospital. As I prepared to leave for home, I noted in my journal that I had certainly been impressed with the genuine caring and professionalism that my day and night nurses had shown. The medical technicians had also been experienced and helpful for the most part. With all of the problems of health care financing, it was good to see that genuine humanity and pride of workmanship were still alive and well in some parts of the health care system. My urologist of three years who did the surgery was as attentive and precise as always.

Despite all the good care, I felt imprisoned by the hospital environment. A big part of that was being stuck in a strange building for four days without any fresh air, and breathing the special smell of latex and germicides that hospitals have. In addition, my own body system was struggling with the remnants of anesthesia and pain medication still in my bloodstream. After a while, even the food tasted and smelled like chemicals. The necessary battle to control and minimize infection makes hospitals not the most environmentally friendly places.

My family was supportive during my hospital stay. Glenda spent a lot of time sitting with me and brought our daughter and two little granddaughters for a visit. Both of my sisters and two brothers, all of whom live out of town, called several times. I felt loved and cared for, and I did not experience much pain. My operation was on a Wednesday, and by Friday I was able to read my Bible, check my e-mail on my laptop computer, and respond to a call from my office. My doctor was cautious and made me stay until Sunday. Harry, my roommate who had had a similar procedure on the same day, got to leave on Saturday. He had a different doctor, who was perhaps more aggressive. Harry, a retired employee of the federal government, had worked on the original implementation of the Head Start program. My consulting company had had a contract providing training and technical assistance to Head Start programs in three states for eight years. So we had a lot to talk about. Harry was perhaps seventy. He had been in the hospital recently for some work on a knee, and he seemed to be well adapted to the hospital routine, but eager to go home as soon as possible.

Part of the procedure for getting ready to leave the hospital was to walk the halls getting exercise. It was a bit jarring, seeing other men in my same condition, pushing their IV stands down the hall. It felt a bit like some odd kind of foot race, with us men circling around the halls of the hospital ward with our IV contraptions. There was one man in particular who seemed really sad. He seemed to have not recovered from the shock of coming face to face with his mortality. He was a relatively younger man like myself, and as we passed in the hall, he shook his head and said, "Isn't this something?" as though he still could not believe that this could happen to him. I smiled sympathetically. I felt sorry for him and blessed that I was in a better and more receptive place, that I was able to make peace with the reality of my finitude.

The day I left the hospital was one of the most peaceful and satisfying days of my life. To be able to eat my own food, lay in my own bed, and sit on our deck with my two-year-old and six-year-old grandchildren; to look at the sky and trees, and to breathe fresh air, was heaven. It was as though time had slowed almost to a stop, and I could taste each drop of the day like it was forever. I remember thinking that I would like to spend the rest of my life like this; savoring the moment, without worry or concern about what would happen next. Perhaps it was partly the lingering effects of my pain medication. But I believe that it was more than that. I felt no pain at all that day (a situation that, unfortunately, did not last). But I have not and never will let go of the desire for that serenity, which was simultaneously like the absence of anxiety, and the total awareness, calm alertness, and enjoyment of the present as a gift from God.

The next day began another phase of my recovery. I would be homebound for four weeks with a catheter—a portable one that fit under my clothes during the day, and a larger one at night. I was not to ride in a car or perform any strenuous physical activity. I was uncomfortable enough that I was not even tempted to disobey my doctor's orders. I had two types of pain to deal with. One was the deep aching pain from the internal surgical wound, and the other was the irritation of having a catheter inserted in that sensitive portion of my anatomy twenty-four hours a day for four weeks. I refused to take anything for pain but Tylenol. I wanted to have my mind clear, rather than being doped up. But I found that it is difficult to live in the moment, when that moment contains physical pain or discomfort.

The spirit of fear is insidious. Throughout my hospitalization, I had no sense of fear or depression, even when my prospects looked worse than expected. I felt confidence and faith that with God's help, I could cope with whatever circumstances I faced. But over the subsequent few weeks, as I moved into the rehabilitation stage of recovery, and I got back into some of my business and household routines, I became more prone to anxiety about one thing or another. It is so easy to slip back into the spirit of fear, in which we unconsciously, and perhaps instinctively, begin to assume the fight or flight response as both an internal mental attitude and as overt behavior.

I pondered that with growing spiritual discipline and greater self-awareness, I could catch myself before proceeding too far down that road. During that period of alienation, I experienced a sense of being out of time. That is, rather than being in time and with each moment, I was killing time and waiting for it to pass. I was experiencing constant pain or discomfort from my operation during that period, and that is what pushed me into that mode of waiting for time to pass, and to feel better.

Gradually the pain subsided as my body healed, and I just had to deal with the irritation and discomfort from the catheter. I grew to seriously dislike the contraption. But finally the day arrived to remove the catheter, and Glenda drove me to my appointment. My doctor had warned me that once the catheter was removed, it would take time to regain bladder control. But that process was still surprisingly difficult. Having to relearn bladder control at age fifty is definitely a lesson in humility. I was pretty well healed now from prostate surgery, my prognosis looked good, and my catheter was removed. Now I just had to learn again how to control those muscles that enabled me to decide when I am ready to use the bathroom. But I counted my blessings. After all, my problem was bladder control, not bowel control. I thought of the people who are quadriplegic and have no control over their bodies. That must be a difficult path. I pondered that ultimately, we must all acknowledge that the power we think we have is illusion, and that we are all subject to the power of the Creator. Even the most powerful people in the world, who may not have had a serious setback or reversal in their life, will one day face death, sickness, and loss of loved ones. The arrogance that such a charmed life can produce will eventually be broken, or at least dented and cracked.

Eventually, as the weeks and months passed, I gradually got drawn back into the vortex of business. I had resolved to free myself from some of the constraints of my business life, but these adjustments were primarily superficial. I no longer wore a suit unless it was absolutely necessary, and I stopped wearing a watch. For a while, I worked mostly from home and only went into the office one or two days a week. But when it came to the big decisions, I followed my previous path. In addition to my longstanding consulting business, in which my employees provided the direct services to clients, I had started a health care billing business, which required my direct regular involvement. I was both the salesperson and the technician. I had two employees in that unit who did the actually billing of accounts, and the costs exceeded the revenue being generated. I therefore had to choose between closing the billing unit, or spending money and time to enhance its customer base.

I decided to push forward with the expansion, though this involved spending a lot of money to purchase another small billing company and transferring the customers to our system. That this was the wrong decision became clear in six months, when I had to shut down the unit anyway, but then at a much greater cost. But the decision would have been wrong even it succeeded on a financial basis, because by its nature, it required an intensive commitment of my time on a daily basis. Staying busy was a way of avoiding anxiety and boredom, but it also prevented me from discovering what I really needed to do. I had been avoiding dealing with this situation for years. On the one hand, I would despair that my work life consisted of activity necessary to make a living, but lacking more profound meaning and satisfaction. On the other hand, the adrenaline rush of keeping busy was preferable to sitting still and facing the anxiety of not knowing what to do.

After the failure of the billing business, I realized that I needed to get back to living by faith, as I did during my illness. This required that I stop initiating projects to fill time. I needed to accept the idea that having time for reflection is blessing and an opportunity to find meaning and purpose in my life. At that time, I was writing a number of proposals for government consulting contracts, which is how I get the business that is my daily bread. It could be a demanding activity, but this time I decided to do it as an exercise in faith. The question was, how do you invest enough time, energy, and creativity to succeed in a highly competitive process, without losing your soul to it?

I worked hard, through daily meditation, Bible study, and prayer to maintain my focus on God and the eternal, even while working intensely on the proposals. I would know that I had crossed the line if the goal of successfully completing the proposal became too important and troubled my spirit. As I make commitments to other participants and begin investing limited funds, the product tends to become too important. But I had matured enough that I was no longer comfortable accepting that discomforting state. So I found myself pulling back, and letting it go, accepting that though I would work hard to complete the product, it was also okay if I did not. It was an interesting dance; more than interesting because my soul hung in the balance.

To sin is to put anything before God. Theologian Rheinhold Niebuhr surmised that various reasons for the decline and decay of civilizations recapitulate ". . . the various types of human sin.

They would fall into the two general categories of the sins of sensuality, and the sins of pride. In the former the freedom of history is denied and men creep back to the irresponsibility of nature. In the latter the freedom of man is overestimated."[24] On the individual level, we each face continually the challenge of making decisions and taking action without succumbing to fear, greed, or hatred, on the one hand, or pride and egotism on the other. This does not mean we should disdain historical existence for a perfect afterlife, but rather we should seek to experience the power and meaning of the spiritual life, even as we engage seriously in the life here and now. In following that path, we ultimately must acknowledge our inability to make life meaningful through our own power. For Christians, humility opens the door to the personal revelation of Jesus as the Christ, the suffering Messiah, who represents the appearance of the eternal within history; and through whom the historical is transcended and simultaneously made profoundly meaningful.

To defeat and overcome death and fear of death is to know beyond doubt that there is a life of the spirit, which is more important than physical life. That is what I think Jesus meant by loving God above all else, with all of our heart, soul, strength, and mind. When we do this, we enter into a joy of God that gives us the strength to overcome the fear of death; and without the fear of death, we enjoy the abundant life.

To show us the way, Jesus had to face death himself, willingly and sacrificially. He overcame death and his disciples saw him again, strengthening their faith and enabling them to in turn face death and choose the life of the Spirit over physical life. Had they not been totally convinced of this, no Christian religion could have developed after Jesus' crucifixion. We can appreciate the depth and power of that experience without concern about the possibility of literal resurrection. For it is overcoming death and the fear of death while we are still alive that results in the surrender of all things material to the ultimacy of God and the life of the Spirit. In doing so, we are transformed.

The fundamental choice is not between physical life and physical death but between spiritual life and spiritual death. The instinctual remnants in our minds and bodies react to perceived threats as a choice between physical life and physical death, whereas the threat to spiritual life is less immediately evident. Which is the illusion: that we are individual beings isolated from, or having only a random relationship to the flux of time, events, and circumstances that surround us? Or that there is a part of us that fits into that flux like part of a jigsaw puzzle, the meaning of which we influence, but can only dimly understand?

When we fully connect with God, we acknowledge the limitation of our atomistic existence and joyfully commit our will to the building of his kingdom. We do this willingly because we finally recognize the difference between abundant life and existence, and we want that abundant life. Abundant life does not necessarily mean a life of ease and prosperity. It may mean the opposite. But we truly come to appreciate what the psalmist means when he says "Better is one day in your court than a thousand elsewhere; I would rather be a doorkeeper in the house of my God than dwell in the tents of the wicked."[25]

two

PRIDE, HOPE AND THE SEARCH FOR MEANING

*"When pride comes, then comes disgrace,
but with humility comes wisdom."*

— PROVERBS 11:2[1]

The Librarian and the Sin of Pride

When my parents bought the house on Laconia Avenue in the Bronx in 1965, just over the line from Mount Vernon, New York, I knew that owning our home was a good thing. But after leaving my small Caribbean island at age twelve, and having finally, after three years, settled into a sense of belonging with my neighborhood and friends in Mount Vernon, the change was disturbing to me. In some ways, I would never again have that sense of belonging to a place. As I had moved from childhood to being a teenager, I had lost that ability to connect with a neighborhood, the way that children do. As a child, fences do not separate you from the other people on your block the way they do when you become a teenager and adult. And the street in front of your house is not just a means of getting from one place to another, but an important place in its own right.

I did eventually get into the street at Laconia Avenue, but by an indirect route. It was not by just wandering around and discovering the other children, or getting to know through play the utility poles and cracks and crevices in the sidewalk, as I did in Mount Vernon. Instead, I finally met a boy in my eleventh grade English class who lived around the corner from me. He had a skateboard, which we would take turns riding in the street. His name was John, and he said his parents were from Spain.

John was the exception. My two close friends, Rick and Michael, were not from my immediate neighborhood. I met them in school, and we socialized by riding the New York City subways down to Central Park to go ice skating in the winter, or just wandering around the streets of New York exploring in the summer.

Evander Childs High School was on Gunhill Road, a short walk from the elevated subway stop named for that street. Flowing with the mass of other students down the broad concrete front steps of the school and down Gunhill Road to the subway or bus was one of the rituals that marked the end our school day. At that time the neighborhood around the school, including the area extending the four or so train stops to the one closest to my house, was a mixture of Jews, Italians, and some African-Americans. I was in the advanced placement classes, and there were only two blacks in any of my classes, Ramona and Rick. Michael, my other close friend, was of Italian background. Ramona was also important to me, but we were really not that close.

Rick and I were close for a while, and would go ice skating in Central Park. He was a tall, muscular, handsome young African-American man, with a great smile and a gold-capped front tooth. He was a good-natured guy, but serious about school, and certainly someone with whom I should have remained in touch. But as has sometimes been my unfortunate habit throughout life, I drifted on to a new friend and didn't reciprocate Rick's efforts to keep our friendship alive.

Ramona was like a dream to me. She was pretty and smart, and the only black girl my age with whom I had regular contact. But since I was painfully shy around girls, we did not become close. We did go together once to see the Broadway show *Man of La Mancha*, but for the most part, we just saw each other in class. I ran into her about ten years after graduation in Cambridge, Massachusetts; she was alone at a festival on the Charles River. I saw her after that once with her husband and children. The last time I saw her was around 1990, when she was on television discussing the work of her recently deceased husband, who was an author and university professor.

Michael was the high school friend who had the most impact on me. He was in my English class in eleventh and twelfth grades. I was the editor-in-chief of the school newspaper during one or both of those years. Working on the newspaper was part of our advanced placement English class. Michael and I had a lot of fun discussing philosophy, going ice-skating, and walking in Central Park. He introduced me to the work of Bertram Russells and others who impressed him. He also was fond of the rock group, the Doors, whose lyrics dripped with existential angst and anger. Michael lived with his mother in the high rise housing project on Gunhill Road, a couple of blocks from the school. We would go over to his house after school and listen to music. He was the leader, and I followed because I could identify with the emotional and intellectual experience that he was having. I was shocked and embarrassed to hear him scream at his mother, often over things that seemed to me inconsequential; but in my much quieter way, I was also incubating the seeds of rebellion.

Michael was part of a loose grouping of boys who were at the upper end of the academic spectrum, and who lived within several train stops of the high school. Most of the others were Jewish, including Alan and Mark. Apparently some of them had known each other for years before they met me. Michael talked about riding rafts with some of them down the small river that ran through the northern part the Bronx, when they were much younger. The other two boys from the group whom I knew the best were Alan and Mark.

I remember Alan first from my Spanish class with Mr. Henderson. Alan was the boy in the group whom I found the most intriguing. He was tall and handsome, so he got attention from the prettiest girls. Alan goofed off a lot. He struck me as being thoughtful and perceptive but with the need to hide his intelligence behind humor and a rebellious, individualistic stance. Alan was sitting behind me and to my right in Mr. Henderson's Spanish class during a test, for which he obviously was not prepared. Alan wanted to look at my answers, and I let him. Mr. Henderson caught us and was angry, particularly with me. When I was older and more socially aware, I realized that Mr. Henderson, who was black, was angry at me because of all of the relative educational and other disadvantages that African-Americans were experiencing, and still experience to this day. But at that time, I had no understanding of these things, and isolated in my almost exclusively white social circle, I was operating under the pleasant delusion that race didn't matter.

Alan and I were never close friends like Michael and I. We didn't call each other up and do things together. He was too socially with-it, and I was too socially naïve for that. Michael was also streetwise, but he did not have the glamour and good looks of Alan. In fact, Michael was a bit of an outcast within the loose group. And that may be why we were compatible. I was this bright, shy, naïve black kid, an object of curiosity among my white classmates, but definitely not one of the guys. Michael and Alan had a competitive relationship, and occasionally in class, they would even briefly square off and throw a few punches at each other.

Recognizing Alan's talent and individualistic approach, our English teacher and newspaper advisor suggested that Alan write a regular column discussing his perspective on issues that he could select. As the editor–in–chief of the paper, I suggested a title for the column that sounded cool to me, but was in fact tired and pseudo-cool, and would have been embarrassing to Alan. It was something like "Al tells it like it is." That is how socially inept I was. Michael quickly agreed with the title and seized on it as a way of embarrassing Alan. Fortunately, the game was stopped before we went to press. Michael was a real friend to me, but he could not let that friendship deprive him of an opportunity to stick it to Alan.

When I was back in the neighborhood during my freshman year of college, I remember having a discussion with Alan and Michael about the psychologist B.F. Skinner's utopian novel *Walden Two*. In that book, Skinner creates a "perfect" society through application of his behavior modification techniques. Michael and I were impressed with the concept and the results presented. But Alan insisted that he would never want to give anyone the power to make those kinds of decisions for him. That's what I meant about his perceptiveness. Alan got right to the central issue: Is it worth giving up freedom to get a peaceful and orderly society? He said no, and today I agree with him, though freedom is now a more complicated concept than the issue of social control. As Thomas Merton states, "Only the man who has rejected all evil so completely that he is unable to desire it at all is truly free."[2] The external evil of totalitarianism, even of a benevolent kind, is easier to recognize and fight than the evil within each of us from which we must struggle to be free; but from which we can ultimately only be freed by the grace of God.

Mark is the only one of the guys from high school whose path I continue to cross periodically. Mark is good-humored and easygoing. We did not have a lot of individual interaction in high school, but he lived not too far from my house, and he was the only one of the group who came to my house and had dinner with me and my family. At the Woodstock festival in 1969, out of five hundred thousand people milling around in the mud and music, who walks right up to me but Mark. I met Mark again about twenty years later when he became a state manager of mental health services in Massachusetts, and I had a company that contracted with the state to operate mental health programs. He worked in Western Massachusetts, the only region of the state in which my company did not operate programs, so we did not get to do business together. We met again in the year 2000 when he was a consultant with the Washington DC Department of Mental Health, and I had moved to the DC metropolitan area. He talked with justifiable pride about his daughter, who was taking a break after college to go into the Peace Corps to work with poor children in a developing country. That was the kind of thing I could see Mark doing, so I understood his pride in his daughter. Mark also told me that Alan had become a lawyer in the New Jersey and New York area.

I had two guardian angels in high school: an older couple, Mr. and Mrs. Joseph. With the exception of Mrs. Kardstadt in history class, whom I felt reduced my grade because she could not believe that a black boy could perform at the level that I did, almost all my teachers treated me well and fairly. The other borderline case was my art teacher, who once looked at something I had constructed and told me bluntly that it showed no artistic ability whatever, but who later asked to take my picture after I was selected for admission to Harvard University. I doubt that his assessment was entirely correct because my art teacher at Harvard later told me I had ability.

But Mr. and Mrs. Joseph tower in my memory over all the other teachers in my high school. Mrs. Joseph was my English teacher in tenth grade, and she did wonderful things for my self-esteem and academic development. She introduced me to Robert Frost and his idea that "good fences make good neighbors," to George Elliot's *Silas Marner,* and to Thomas Hardy's *Return of the Native.* These and other books helped me to understand that the struggle for identity, and between good and evil that I experienced both internally and in society, was universal. She also took apparent delight in the silly short stories I would write for her assignments.

Mr. Joseph was my guidance counselor, and also sometimes taught a class in which he tried without much success to introduce us to "culture," such as the time he played Stravinsky's *Firebird Suite* in class. We were equally unsuccessful at convincing Mr. Joseph that Aretha Franklin's music was "culture." Despite these mutual cultural limitations, Mr. Joseph was a loving teacher and counselor, who seriously applied himself to the task of helping us make something of our lives. I can still picture the way he held his glasses in one hand, his face expressing both thoughtfulness and kindness, as he conveyed the wisdom of his experience on some topic that he thought would be helpful to us.

For me in particular, I know that Mr. Joseph went beyond the usual counseling about college entrance exams and college selection. For example, he tried to get me to go on an overseas summer student work program, where I could become familiar with another culture. I forget what country it was. But having moved from the Caribbean to the New York area six years earlier, I yearned for stability and hated the idea of traveling. Mr. Joseph also helped me to get a clerical job on Wall Street for the summer after graduation, and he helped me to deal with two crises that occurred toward the end of my high school career. God bless you, Mr. and Mrs. Joseph, and all the other teachers who shepherd children and young people toward adulthood, with kindness, diligence, and high standards.

The crisis of the library book became an issue not only for me but also for the principal and school administration. For me, in retrospect, it highlights my stubborn pride, my inability to recognize when I needed help, and my failure to seek it when it was so available. In addition to being editor of the school newspaper, I was either president or vice president of the graduating class. I don't remember how I got selected for, or elected to the latter, and I don't remember much responsibility being involved in the position. But in addition, I was the third highest ranked student out of a class of more than eight hundred, and I was used to seeing only A's on my report cards. That was before a librarian, whom I may have had for a study period, took it upon herself to put a devastating grade, either a "D" or an "F" (I can't remember which) on my report card, because I had not returned a book on time.

I was outraged. I felt that my motives had been good, and that the punishment was disproportionate to any guilt that I may have been deservedly assigned. It never occurred to me to simply go to Mr. Joseph and get his help in resolving the problem. Instead I did the most outrageous and stupid thing. I erased the mark from my report card. This created a real dilemma for the principal. Here was this lone African-American kid near the top of his class, a goody two shoe who was a poster boy for student achievement and for his race, now committing a capital school offense: falsifying his report card. Thankfully, Mr. Joseph was able to work it out. They recognized that what the teacher had done was also not right. They made it clear that I had really screwed up, but that I would not be punished for it beyond being called to the principal's office and reprimanded. I was scared to death and thankful to have survived the ordeal. The grade was corrected, and I moved on to my next crisis.

This was to be my final hurdle in high school, but it foreshadowed the years of wandering and confusion that would come later with dropping out of college. The top three students in my graduating class were Christine, Gary, and me, in that order. The time had come to decide which two of us would make speeches at graduation. This would ordinarily have gone by default to Christine and Gary, but for one thing, Christine was very shy. I was shy, but Christine was shy-squared. She simply would not get up on that stage. Me, I would be terrified, but I would stand up and give the speech, as if in a dream. I had things to say, usually something depressing and deep, springing from the constant internal struggle I experienced. So Gary was to give the valedictorian address, and I the salutatorian address. We practiced giving our speeches in front of a panel of teachers and met their approval.

Then suddenly, a few days before graduation, I ran into some obscure internal existential objection to giving my speech. As I remember, it was not fear of making the speech, but an ethical objection, something to the effect that since I did not have a genuine relationship with my graduating class, it would be false of me to get up and make a speech to them. I cannot make sense today of what I was experiencing then. But I know that it was heartfelt and genuine. This problem caused a flurry of consultation between Mr. Joseph and my mother, and conversations between each of them and me focused on getting me to change my mind. In the end, I yielded to the pressure of their tag team and agreed to make the speech. It was my usual turgid existential angst; this time about the need to overcome the fear that controls us in order to become fully ourselves. Today, I understand that I was grappling with issues of genuine significance.

Something in me was breaking and falling apart as I graduated from high school. My adolescent rebellion was delayed but would not be denied. I had always been slow when it came to social and physical development, and this pattern continued to hold true.

The Inner Voice

Sitting on my bed, alone in my room, in the quasi-communal off-campus group housing near Harvard Square in Cambridge, Massachusetts, I was overcome with fear and dread for no apparent reason, as sometimes happened when I was alone. It was the beginning of sophomore year, and I was lost and without meaningful direction. The old identity based on excelling in academic performance had died as high school ended, and I was left with question marks and vague impulses. I desired to find something that was real and true in me, that could direct me to my place in the world. The fear had always lurked not far beneath the mask of conformity, but now, as the mask disintegrated, only fear was left.

I was certainly not the only one experiencing something like this. My roommate Nick, my best friend from freshman year, was also lost in his own state of depression and alienation. He had been so confident last year. Then, at the end of the school year, he had a "bad trip" on LSD or something similar, and he had not regained his confidence. I had also had my own "bad trip," which was an intense heightened state of fear and panic. But once the drug wore off, I did not change perceptibly. That is perhaps because I had never been confident to begin with. I knew my fear. It was an almost constant companion, usually held at bay, but not totally out of awareness. We were both marooned on our own islands and unable to reach out and support each other. Instead, I brought into our room some of the hippie kids I had met hanging out in Harvard Square the summer after freshman year. This was the group that I would live with for about eight months after I dropped out of college.

But now I was alone in our room and overwhelmed with fear. This time I didn't run to find someone to distract me from my fear. Something within me said to sit still and I would be all right. So I sat as my fear intensified, and then, amazingly, it passed, and I felt warmed and comforted by the assurance that I was not alone, that I had a path, and I just had to have faith and follow it wherever it led. And at that moment, I knew that I would leave school, and live day to day, without any plans for the future; but just to always listen closely to the voice within. It wasn't really a voice like a hallucination. Rather, it was the same experience of serenity and faith that I have today when I am in deep prayer or meditation. It's a surrender of the planning, controlling, wishing, hoping, and regretting to just being in the present and connecting to the source of creativity and being. At that time, I did not interpret this experience in Christian terms at all, but more in vaguely Zen terms. I was reading a science fiction book at that time by Robert Heinlein, about a Buddha-like extraterrestrial who comes to earth. My experiences then left me with an unarticulated sense that there was a path that I needed to follow. And to stay on that path, I needed to maintain a somewhat detached and unemotional stance as I participated in life events.

In addition to dropping out of college, the other outward expression of the inward change was that I began to play music. I got a pair of bongo drums and a simple wooden flute, and playing these became my most consistent organized activity. This was not really a goal-oriented activity aimed at mastering the instruments. It was more ritualistic and aimed at inducing and maintaining that spiritual state I had first experienced alone in my room. Later, it developed a social component as I learned to play with guitar-playing friends over the course of the next three years. But I did not begin studying music formally and taking lessons until about four years later, when I began to consider returning to college. It was my experience of working as an aide in a McLean psychiatric hospital just outside of Boston, that reawakened my interest in academic learning and the desire to return to college.

I did not relate this first adult spiritual experience, of having a real internal life and connectedness to a guiding presence that transcended myself, to my childhood experiences of Christianity. And to that extent it was an experience disembodied from the cultural and social moorings of my life. It matched my then current alienation from my family and separation from African-American and Afro-Caribbean social life. My re-identification with these roots first came through playing and listening to music. Then eventually the desire to be part of that community again became irresistible. Once I rejoined that community, the Christian spiritual experience and the music fit into one social whole, but connecting these to my internal spiritual experience would take decades of trial and error.

The Accidental Psychologist

I used to have a recurring dream of the white wooden Moravian church of my childhood in St. Kitts. The dreams were always about struggling to get to this place of clarity, security, and strength. Without much reflection, I accepted this as natural; that at its core, my ultimate concern was spiritual and was aptly represented as a church. But it was surprising when I had a similar dream about a psychiatric hospital, McLean Hospital.

The dream was more like a moment of revelation than a story or set of scenes. It was like the answer to a question. The answer came in sensations, images, and words: the words were "food and light." The question was something like: "Why is this place important?" I interpreted this to mean that McLean Hospital had provided me sustenance and knowledge, and had set me on the path to becoming myself. This was despite the fact that at least twice I had rebelled against the place, and made myself persona non grata among the powers that be there, ultimately leading to my leaving permanently to seek greener pastures.

A person builds a life and an identity by bringing to the task his or her key personal experiences, both positive and negative, with people and places. McLean Hospital in Belmont, Massachusetts, the flagship of Harvard Medical School's Psychiatry Department, played such a role in my professional and personal development. This is so true that in the year 2000, fifteen years after having regular contact with that institution, I could have one of those profound revelatory dreams about the place.

The dream also touched on the point that my first job at McLean was as an aide in the food service department, or more precisely as a dishwasher and general cleanup person. I first went to McLean in the fall of 1972. At that time, I had dropped out of Harvard University two years earlier, and had spent that summer working with a house painting company called Fat and Frosty, composed of fellow Harvard dropouts and graduates. Now that the house painting season was over, I needed a job. A newspaper ad led me to apply at McLean.

The hospital sat up on a hill a short distance from a square where the trackless trolley from Cambridge stopped, and where there was a bank branch, a small number of stores, and a restaurant called Andros Diner. The hospital, at that time, consisted of a number of buildings spread out over a large area with fields of neatly mowed grass, woods, streets, and parking lots. There were two ways to get up the hill to the administration building. If you were driving, you would follow the street around to the main hospital entrance and take the driveway through the apple orchard up to the parking lot in front of the administration building. If you were walking or riding a bike, you could take a more direct steep paved path from the street up through the woods, across the fields of manicured grass up to the same parking lot. I believe that first day in 1972, I didn't know about the shortcut, and ended up walking the longer route.

In the personnel department, I had my interview with a friendly young man who seemed embarrassed that he could not offer me anything more than a dishwasher job. We talked about music (I played the flute), and he recalled someone playing the song "The Girl From Epanema" on the flute at a wedding. We had a good conversation, and he suggested I take the food service job, come back to him after a few months, and see what else was available.

My most memorable experience in the food service department was working with a mentally retarded employee who lived at the nearby Fernald School. This man, whom I will call Dave, got on everyone's nerves because he talked repeatedly about the same thing. The topic was generally about his problems with an actual or potential girlfriend, and a phrase he used repeatedly was "I lost out." At that point in time, I did not even know the difference between mental retardation and mental illness, but our supervisor found that I had a greater degree of patience with Dave than did our fellow workers, so we ended up working together a great deal. I do recall, however, that I once lost patience with him and yelled at him. I felt badly about it and never did it again.

While working in the food service department, I ran into a female social worker or social work intern, whom I had met at a small mental health counseling agency. She made a joke of my job (or me), talking about how I was cleaning up for that other agency, and now I was cleaning up for McLean. Somehow, her attitude gave me the impression that she thought I was destined to do nothing but mop floors and wash dishes for the rest of my life. I frankly did not know what I was destined for. I had jumped off the academic track and jeopardized my scholarship to Harvard, because I needed to find out what I wanted to do rather than just following the path laid out for me. True, I was part of a poor black immigrant family from the Caribbean, and the first in my immediate family to attend college, but those economic realities could not deter me from my seemingly foolhardy quest for self-discovery. I was not willing to go back to school until I found something I really wanted to study and know.

At that time, I had an interest in music. I had taught myself to play the flute after a fashion, but had not taken lessons. I just played by ear, by myself, and with folk guitar players. My lifelong passion for reading continued, mostly in the form of science fiction books and other fiction. Musically, I was listening to Rahsaan Roland Kirk, the popular jazz flutist and saxophone player. My tastes were shifting from rock to jazz. I was searching, but still pretty alienated from myself—a stranger in a strange land.

Working in the cafeteria gave me the chance to observe the staff and patients who all came in shifts to eat meals. I became interested in learning what was happening on the wards or units. After a few months, I went back to my friend in personnel and asked for a job as a mental health worker on one of the units. After being interviewed in the cafeteria by the unit nursing director, I was hired as a mental health worker on the NB2 unit. The chief psychiatrist of NB2 was Philip Kelleher, a charismatic neo-Freudian who talked in riddles and metaphors, and had his own approach to understanding and treating mental illness.

Dr. Kelleher was committed to teaching his staff and held seminars on the unit, based on assigned reading. These seminars, in addition to staff meetings, unit meetings with patients, case conferences, co-leading patient group therapy, and case management of assigned patients, were my first real experience in psychology. I had taken an introductory psychology course freshman year, but that had no more meaning to me than anything else in school at that time. Under Dr. Kelleher's tutelage, I became intellectually engaged and challenged for the first time since high school. My year and a half at Harvard did not count since I had already mentally dropped out by the time I arrived there.

With my awakened interest in psychology, I began to read more broadly: philosophical novelists such as Tolstoy, Dostoyevsky, Thomas Mann; psychological biographies by Erik Erikson of Martin Luther and others; and eventually psychological-oriented philosophy and social analysis by Kierkegaard and Frantz Fanon. Eventually I returned to school, but to Berklee College of Music, rather than back to Harvard University. My scholarships to Harvard had expired, and in any case, I would not have been able to study music there. So, I spent three years completing a degree at Berklee while continuing to work sixteen hours per week as a mental health worker at McLean Hospital.

Because of my limited experience playing a musical instrument, music school was at times frustrating and depressing. But despite my limited technical skills, I was able to learn the theoretical and intellectual side of music readily, and able to experience deep appreciation for jazz, classical music, ragtime, and traditional African music. After finishing my undergraduate degree in music, I entered an expressive therapy program at Lesley College. The program sought to use music and other arts as part of the therapeutic mental health process. I found that the only part of that program that held my interest were the courses taught by a child psychologist and a neuropsychologist.

After I began working as a counselor to elderly people living alone, my supervisor, who was a psychology graduate student, suggested that I consider applying to the clinical psychology program at Boston University, and gave me a professor to contact. I spent six months in my own self-study program learning all the psychology I never had in college in order to do well on the Graduate Record Examination. I applied successfully to the Boston University clinical psychology program and left the expressive therapy program after the first year.

Return to Church

I am not sure what precipitated my return to church. It began in my first year of psychology graduate school and lasted about two years. I joined St. Paul's African Methodist Episcopal Church in Cambridge, Massachusetts. During that time, I not only attended Sunday services, but also Bible study during the week. I also actively participated in some of the church groups. On my own, I read through the New Testament books of Matthew, Mark, Luke, and John, and also fasted on at least one occasion. As I read the Bible and participated in church service, I felt close to something very real and very important in my life. But I still had these intellectual doubts, and nothing I heard could put the pieces together to my satisfaction.

After about two years, I just drifted away from the church. I don't recall making a decision about it. It just sort of happened. I didn't think much about religion again until seventeen years later, at age forty-seven. Why was something that now seems so obvious so difficult to put together? The short answer is that I did not have the conceptual framework to fit my life experiences and intellect into Christian theology, and no one I met in the context of church was able to give me one. Though I experienced the emotive and symbolic power of the Scripture as I read it alone, and the worship services, I could not accept or make sense of the literal interpretations provided by my church leaders; and I did not have an alternative way of reconciling these conflicts myself.

So I drifted back out the door, into a life of pursuing technical knowledge and mastery of my small part of the material world. Only failure to find satisfaction in the material world by midlife would instigate the spiritual crisis that would force me to search again for my inner voice. And this time all of the pieces of my life and personality had to be put together.

One of the things I promised my wife when we relocated to Maryland was that I would attend church with her regularly. That's how it began. But as I attended church, I began to experience the meaning of the biblical message as significant to my struggle to make sense of my life. This struggle had intensified beginning at about age forty-five. I had been working through it primarily using concepts and experiences from psychology.

I used to puzzle about these matters about the beginning, end, and infinity of the universe when I was a boy. Even then I knew that scientific knowledge, while important, would never ultimately answer these questions. We will always learn more and more, and the horizon will always remain in the distance as we approach it. It also used to depress me, when I was about twenty years old, to think that the lifespan of even planets and suns are finite. This made me feel that life is somehow futile. At that time I also believed in reincarnation. This does not bother me anymore, and I no longer believe in reincarnation. I accept the limitation of my lifespan and that of other entities and objects, even suns and planets. That does not in any way decrease for me the importance of how I live my life. I have relinquished the need for physical immortality. But through a greater connectedness with the important people in my life, with my work, with the Holy Spirit, and with music and the works of others, I attain a sense of another kind of immortality.

Finding Hope Among the Hopeless

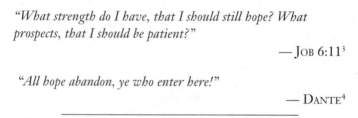

"What strength do I have, that I should still hope? What prospects, that I should be patient?"

— JOB 6:11[3]

"All hope abandon, ye who enter here!"

— DANTE[4]

Bridgewater State Hospital, the maximum security mental hospital for the state of Massachusetts, is about a forty-five-minute drive south of Boston. It is located in a large complex that also has separate facilities and grounds for a medium-security prison and a treatment center for sexual offenders. This massive complex is the only apparent industry in the small exurban town after which the facility is named, and through which one has to drive going to and from it. The last stretch is a long, narrow, straight two-way road; a speed trap that invites you to exceed the speed limit, and to add to another source of revenue for the municipality. Just as you are zipping down that road, you come to an easily missed turnoff, with a small sign naming the place as Massachusetts Correctional Institution (MCI) Bridgewater.

The turnoff is a narrow paved road through the woods. There is no gate here. As you pass the main sign at the entrance, there is another small sign that warns of dire consequences for trespassing. This second sign always reminded me of the sign in a novel by Herman Hesse, quoted from Dante: "All hope abandon, ye who enter here!" Driving down that narrow wooded road is a transitional stage, in which you leave behind the normal life of a small town with neat houses and lawns and emerge into another world of razor wire fences, guard towers, and men in uniforms. Those in blue are the guards, those in grays or dungaree are the prisoners or patients, and those in civilian clothing are the psychologists, psychiatrists, social workers, and nurses.

All are locked in, for varying durations; some by choice, others by the decisions of others. All are human, and therefore within each one, the struggle between good and evil rages. However, some have acted out that evil in extreme acts of violence, while others may not have done much more than entertain an unkind thought or an illicit fantasy. Among those who have committed violent acts, some have done so for the usual range of criminal motives such as passion, profit, or power. Others have acted under the influence of various delusions and auditory hallucinations, the result of thought and mood disturbances, which cloud the usual distinctions between fantasy and reality, between right and wrong, and between choice and compulsion.

A psychologist named Wes drove me to Bridgewater that first trip in 1980. He was my predecessor, as the lone African-American psychologist negotiating the boundaries between Harvard-affiliated McLean Hospital and the Massachusetts prison system. I learned a lot from Wes, as much from watching him as from talking with him. As we drove on this first day, we talked about the Association of Black Psychologists, in which we had both been involved, though at different levels and in different locations.

I had never been inside a prison. I had also never been in a state mental hospital. My only related experience was from working for about six of the previous eight years at McLean Hospital, with its rolling lawns and tennis courts. Bridgewater State Hospital looked more like a prison than a hospital to me. The razor wire fences and guard towers commanded the view from the adjacent parking lot. In its middle, the fence facing the parking lot turned in upon itself at right angles, forming a short passageway that led to the front door. This front door opened into a small anteroom where those desiring entry had to appeal to the entrance guard inside a bulletproof glass cage. This is where a determination was made as to who and what could enter based on the established rules. Meeting that criteria, you then entered the first electronically locked metal door to another chamber, where you walked through the metal detector, as the first door locked behind you. If that went well, the guard pushed a button unlocking the second metal door, releasing you into the administration building.

I went to Bridgewater by choice, and with a lot of intense interest, generated by some previous experiences with violence. In 1978, the year before I began the psychology graduate program at Boston University, there were a series of murders of African-American women in Boston that led to a general state of alarm and meetings and demonstrations in the black community. A group of young women, mostly single women with children, led by a middle-aged woman who had a history of community activism, formed a group that met regularly at the Harriet Tubman House. They sought to mobilize and focus community reaction to the killings. I had been seeking a meaningful way of getting involved in the black community and began attending their meetings and participating in their events. I was the first man in the group, but later other young men and women, who had histories of social activism in college, in labor unions, and in past community issues joined us.

The killings stopped, but the cases were never solved. The women who had started the group eventually went back to their regular lives of working and taking care of their children, but the younger men and women, including myself, soon coalesced around another crisis in the black community: the police shooting of a young black man under suspicious circumstances. We organized demonstrations in front of the local courthouse, which was just around the corner from the local police station, and were successful in bringing media attention to the case.

These activities had long-term effects on my life. This group, some of whom had known each other from college, became my friends and main peer group for several years. Through the meetings, I met my first wife, to whom I was briefly married for less than two years. And through one of these friends, I met Glenda, to whom I have been married now for eighteen years. In addition, as I proceeded with my graduate studies in clinical and community psychology, my experiences of community activism, precipitated by the killing of several black women and a teenage boy, stirred my desire to understand violence, its causes, and what can be done to prevent it.

This interest led me, during my second year in graduate school, to do a practicum (pre-internship placement) at Bridgewater State Hospital. Although called a state hospital, Bridgewater was run by the Massachusetts Department of Correction, not the Department of Mental Health. McLean Hospital, where I had had my first introduction to mental health and mental illness in 1972, and where I had worked until 1977, had at this time two contracts with the corrections department. One was to provide psychiatrists, psychologists, and clinical social workers to Bridgewater, and another was to provide mental health services in the prisons themselves. The goal was to maintain mentally ill prisoners in the prisons when possible, and to send only the most severely ill to Bridgewater.

It only recently occurred to me that a more personal motivation for going to Bridgewater might have been to understand my own father. He was a man with an unpredictable and violent temper, at least in his relationship with my mother. His other side was being an independent craftsman, businessman, and family provider. He ran his own house painting business, and I actually worked one job with him and his crew. His death, when I was ten years old, had both elements of violence and work ethic. He and a co-worker were killed by a train while painting railroad signs in England.

I stayed at Bridgewater for five years, moving from the role of psychology practicum student to an intern; then after completing my dissertation research there, I worked as a clinical psychologist, evaluator and expert witness, and a unit clinical administrator. Each workday, I joined others in the ritual entry past the guard in the bulletproof room and through the electronic locked double doors and the metal detector.

On the other side from the entrance, the administration building opened on a large rectangular courtyard, which was enclosed by razor wire fences. Other buildings were arranged around its inside perimeter. Guard towers rose at each corner. The structure directly across from the administration building housed the cafeteria, school, and recreation facilities. The cycles of daily institutional life were marked by the regularly scheduled counts of patients in each unit, and by the members of each unit filing across the quad for meals in their appointed turn. In good weather, the patients who were not restricted could gather on the quad to smoke cigarettes, socialize, and watch the seagulls that sometimes flew overhead. And even though the sun shone at Bridgewater like anywhere else, there was another kind of weather that was constant within its borders—a grayness matching the patients' uniforms; and a heaviness that hung over the place, reflecting the deathly serious acts that often preceded a patient's entry into the facility, and their reflection in the delusions and hallucinations that continued to haunt them.

As you walked out of the administration building, the two maximum security units, Max 1 and Max 2, stood on the righthand side of the quad. Max 2 was the unit where I was stationed for most of my tenure at Bridgewater. Renata was the psychologist directing the clinical care of patients on Max 2 when I arrived.

She was also director of clinical training, and I therefore was put under her supervision for both reasons. Max 2 housed the patients requiring the most supervision and care because of the symptoms of their mental illness, combined with a history of violence. But these men were still generally able to move around their unit and walk to the cafeteria. The men who were in the most extreme condition were confined to the seclusion unit or the medical unit, both of which were located conveniently next to Max 2.

Max 1 was the unit where prisoners, who could not be maintained in other correctional facilities because of mental illness, were evaluated and treated. In contrast, the Max 2 admissions usually came from the court system or from the state mental health system. The expected natural progression was for the men to move from the Max units to one of the six minimum units across the quad, hopefully without retrogressing to seclusion or the medical unit.

I found some of the correctional officers on Max 2 to be strikingly caring and decent men. I remember in particular Al, Dick, and John. These officers had to deal with the physical needs of men who were disturbed and potentially violent on a daily basis. They ensured that their patients were cleaned and fed, restrained them when necessary, and took them to the seclusion unit. The officers sometimes got injured in the process. They dealt with all of this with a surprising combination of humor and gruff but fatherly attention. Al also participated in a therapy group that Renata led comprised of about six patients. This benevolent attitude in the face of real danger was in sharp contrast to the more stereotypical attitudes of the group of officers who worked the evening and night shifts. These latter viewed the patients as prisoners only, to be treated with suspicion and to be kept at a distance. On some units, there were longstanding rumors of patient abuse or at least questionable behavior by officers.

My role as a psychologist at Bridgewater was an ambivalent one, from the perspective of the patients. On the one hand, I was there to provide and manage their treatment; but on the other, I had to evaluate them and provide expert witness to the court about their fitness to leave the facility and go to back to jail, prison, or the state mental health system. Their destination depended on the circumstances and legal statute under which they were admitted. Each week, the judges would convene court in the administration building, and the psychologists and psychiatrists would have to testify about the mental health and "dangerousness" of the patients we knew and worked with regularly.

We were doctors and healers, but also jailers and protectors of the public, though we did not carry keys to the facility. This is the situation of clinical staff at any mental health facility where patients are kept involuntarily, but the security role was highlighted by the severe nature of this particular facility. Despite their security role, clinical staff were rarely the targets of physical or verbal assault from the patients at Bridgewater. One of the riskier times for us was when we had to tell a patient that we would have to recommend to the judge that he stay at Bridgewater. We were usually cautious in doing this to avoid directly confronting the delusions of a psychotic patient with a history of violence.

On one occasion, I was not cautious enough. It may have been lack of sleep the previous night, or perhaps I was distracted by something going on in my personal life. I don't remember the specific cause, but I do remember feeling somewhat off-center that day. The patient was a man who believed that he was Jesus Christ. I called him into the interview office on his unit and asked him to sit down across the desk from me. On his side of the desk, he had direct access to the door, which I left open. In these positions, he could block my access to the door, but this was safer than my blocking his access. If he got agitated, it was safer for both of us if it was easy for him to leave, as opposed to him feeling trapped in the room with me.

In interviewing a patient, the doctor could request the presence of an officer if one judged it necessary, but this was not done on a routine basis. Generally, the door was left open, and the officers were out on the unit, hopefully within earshot. So, the patient and I sat down across the desk from each other, and I told him that I would have to recommend to the judge that he remain at Bridgewater. I had done this numerous times without incident, but this time I misjudged the patient. Before I even knew what was happening, he grabbed me, we scuffled, he hit me, and then he rushed out of the room. As I tried to pull myself together, the social worker came in and asked if I was okay. I was fortunate; only my pride was seriously hurt. The patient was escorted by the officers to the seclusion unit.

In some ways, this was a typical incident of a patient losing control and getting put into seclusion. However, it was unusual because assaults on clinical staff were rare; and in fact, physical assaults on anyone were not as frequent as might be expected. I had the opportunity to examine this issue closely at least for the members of the Bridgewater population who were from the prison system, who were not diagnosed as psychotic, and who were not mentally retarded. Admittedly, this was a somewhat atypical subgroup who were at Bridgewater for evaluation, but were not obviously severely mentally ill. I selected this group because I wanted to understand how institutional "rule-breaking behavior" including insubordination, contraband, verbal harassment, stealing, and physical assault, was related to the social and moral attitudes and backgrounds of prisoners in Bridgewater.[5]

By this time in my tenure at Bridgewater, I understood how a delusional and psychotic person could commit single or multiple murders, often of family members or other important people in the patient's life. But I also knew that most murders and other violence were not done by mentally ill people. So I was more interested in understanding the moral thinking and attitudes of the relatively "normal people" who do most of the killing and other crimes.

I went through the institutional research approval procedure of McLean Hospital, the contractor who was my actual employer as an intern, as well as those of the department of correction. Participation was voluntary and consisted of interviews in which I administered standard psychological tests, as well as tests of social and moral attitudes. The test that I was the most interested in was the one for Machiavellianism. In his books *The Prince* and *The Discourses*, Niccolo Machiavelli, a sixteenth century Italian diplomat, describes the ruthless measures a ruler must apply in order to unify Italy, which then existed as independent city-states. Machiavelli used as his model a much-despised tyrant of Northern Italy named Caesar Borgia.

The Machiavellianism scale was published by psychologists Richard Christie and Florence Geis in 1970. It is a questionnaire that asks subjects to rate the extent to which they agree or disagree with statements derived from *The Prince* and *The Discourses*.[6] This includes cynical statements such as "Most people forget more easily the death of a parent than the loss of their property" and "The biggest difference between most criminals and other people is that criminals are stupid enough to get caught." Essentially, it endorses a moral philosophy that converts Jesus' "Do unto others as you would have them do unto you" into " Do it to others before they can do it to you."

The main finding of my Bridgewater study was that those prisoners who rated high on Machiavellianism were more likely to break the rules within the institution. This is consistent with the common sense notion that people who despise other people and the rules of society are more likely to break those rules. What surprised me was to discover that the level of Machiavellianism of these prisoners as a group was no higher than those of a group of businesspeople. In their lab experiments, Richard Christie and Florence Geis found that the people who performed better in various competitive tasks were higher in Machiavellianism. So the difference between many successful people and criminals may have more to do with opportunity than with morals.

In a perhaps extreme example, an educated thief has opportunities to embezzle money or to manipulate stocks, but an uneducated thief has opportunities only for burglary or armed robbery. The uneducated thief is more likely to be caught during a burglary or armed robbery involving relatively small amounts of money, and is more likely to physically harm or kill someone in the process, leading to graver consequences. The educated thief may not only not be caught, but he may be canonized in the business press as a financial genius. And when he finally is caught, the corporate criminal will likely pay a fine or be sent to a "country-club" prison, rather than doing hard time.

The corporate striver and the underclass survivor both face temptation. Operating under very different circumstances, each still must make decisions about right and wrong. For the survivor, the temptation is that the opportunities are too limited. This then justifies breaking the rules and taking what you can get, because the whole game seems unfair. For the striver, the temptation is that opportunities are plentiful, and the line between "a smart tough business decision" and doing wrong can be made to seem academic. The law favors the corporate striver, but in the eyes of God, they are equally responsible. Most of us don't commit either street crime or corporate crime, but we struggle with good and evil every day. The object of our temptation may be legal, and it may be invisible to every other human being. But "all have sinned and fall short of the glory of God . . ."[7]

I said earlier that I had come to have a good understanding of the type of Bridgewater patient who had killed one or more people in a psychotic and delusional state associated with schizophrenia. But what took me longer to understand is how these men, who lived so far from the mainstream of humanity and were cut off both physically and psychologically from everyday social interactions and relationships, could still find hope. When stabilized on their medications, they were able to participate in Renata's therapy group. I was in the group as her trainee and assistant. We did not talk about their delusions or about their violence. Instead, we talked about the small challenges and victories of everyday life, even life in an institution.

At Bridgewater, having a good day might mean being able to march across the yard with the other patients from Max 2 to go to lunch, rather than being restricted to the unit or being in the seclusion unit. I remember one group meeting in particular, in which Job's question seemed to hang in the air, perhaps unspoken, but somehow understood by us as a group: "What strength do I have, that I should still hope? What prospects, that I should be patient?" And I am amazed and humbled that the men who spoke were able to find something to hope for. Both the older man, who had had so many episodes and peaks and valleys in the course of his illness, and the young man, who had some kind of doomsday delusion that led him to take violent action, joined with the others, Renata, and me in gratefully finding our footing on some small island of hope there at the ends of the earth, while all sense and reason shouted, "All hope abandon, ye who enter here!"[8]

The Holy Ghost in the Gun Tower

> "*The Holy Spirit is the spirit of God indwelling in man. But this indwelling Spirit never means a destruction of human self-hood. There is therefore a degree of compatibility and continuity between human self-hood and the Holy Spirit. Yet the Holy Spirit is never a mere extension of man's spirit or identical with its purity and unity in the deepest or highest levels of consciousness.*"
>
> — REINHOLD NIEBUHR[9]

The maximum security prison in Massachusetts used to be called Massachusetts Correctional Institution (MCI) Walpole, named after the small pretty exurban town of Walpole where it is located. In the 1990s, the name of the prison was changed to MCI Cedar Junction, probably because the people of Walpole got tired of having their attractive town associated with the state's most notorious prison. In the summer of 1981, after my first academic year as a psychology trainee at Bridgewater State Hospital, I worked as a clinician at MCI Cedar Junction. I was an employee in the prison mental health services contract then held by McLean Hospital. It was during that time, on a day when I was the only mental health clinician in the prison, that an armed guard in one of the towers became incoherent and unresponsive to commands from his supervisors.

The high white walls of MCI Cedar Junction rose like a cement castle from grassy fields and occasional smaller buildings along the two-lane road that led from the center of Walpole to the prison. The administration building, which opened onto the parking lot, was actually outside the main prison compound, so that one could walk through the front door and into the building almost like a regular public building. The security started once you got into the administration building. To get to the main prison building, you passed through a metal detector and several heavily reinforced steel doors, operated by guards in rooms with bulletproof glass. You also walked through a passageway, in which you could be observed by a guard from above as you crossed over to the main prison building.

In a strictly enforced dress code, only prisoners were allowed to wear anything resembling blue jeans. One day, I wore a pair of pants that were not blue jeans, but apparently were close enough in color to concern the guards. So I was given a pair of khaki pants to wear for that day, in order to be allowed into the prison. The main prison building was one big corridor, with cell blocks, a cafeteria, and the health unit at right angles along the corridor, and the segregation units at each end. Sounds were amplified and bounced off the concrete and steel as though the building was one big echo chamber.

The health unit had a corridor for mental health, which consisted of a couple of interview rooms and a handful of cells where prisoners could be kept for observation, while we determined whether their transfer to Bridgewater State Hospital was necessary. On most days, I worked with Tom, who was an experienced clinical social worker and the on-site mental health manager. On some days, we were joined by a psychiatrist, who prescribed psychiatric medication for mentally ill prisoners when needed, and followed those on medication through periodic interviews. The three of us would go out to lunch at a nearby restaurant, and the psychiatrist, who was a collector of rare books, would show us catalogs of books that he was interested in, and discuss the pricing and other issues of great interest only to collectors. Being the newcomer to the prison mental health services and still training to be a psychologist, I accepted the lunch ritual as just another part of the professional culture.

After I had learned the routine of mental health activities in the prison, I began to work alone on days when Tom was either at another facility or not working. The routine consisted of interviewing prisoners in the mental health area and visiting men in the two segregation units, who were on medication or otherwise under our care. A mental health review could be conducted at the request of prisoners or officials. Less frequently, we would have a prisoner on suicide watch or other observation in one of the cells in the mental health unit. If someone needed to be transferred to Bridgewater State Hospital, we would page Wes, who was the director of the mental health program and a licensed psychologist.

One day, I was sitting in the office in the mental health unit, when an officer asked me to report to the administration building for an emergency. When I got there, I learned that an officer in one of the guard towers had been acting strangely, and not responding to his supervisors. As was customary, he had a rifle with him in the tower, and that increased their concern. His responses to them seemed to be incoherent, and he also seemed to be continually praying to God. They had no idea what to do, and I was out of my depth. I appeared professional, because I automatically asked the kinds of questions I was taught to ask in order to make a basic assessment of a crisis situation, but I had no plan to get him down from the tower.

We discussed having someone approach the tower and attempt to talk to him from the ground, since he was not answering the phone. I remember my fear and apprehension that I might be expected to do this. I did go outside with someone else and try to assess the situation from a distance, but I did not go close to the tower. I was saved from having to make that decision by a chaplain (or perhaps he was a lay minister of some sort for he was not wearing a collar). He was already positioned at the foot of the tower and was trying to talk with the officer. Speaking to the guard from a spiritual perspective seemed to enable communication. He eventually came down from the tower and walked with the minister back to the administration building.

Once the officer was out of the tower, the prison administrators then turned to the issue of what to do with him. They requested that I interview him. He was a young African-American man, about thirty years old. As I sat with him, he continued to pray, his prayers sprinkled with exclamations of "Thank you Jesus." His facial expressions and tears indicated an intense and ecstatic spiritual experience. If we had been in church, his behavior would have been perfectly understandable to me. Other worshippers would have simply recognized that he was filled with the Holy Spirit and would have responded with complementary expressions and physical support, if necessary to keep him safe. But there, in the prison situation, I could not make sense of his behavior. Was this a psychotic episode induced by long periods of isolation up in the tower, or a manifestation of a disorder such as schizophrenia or depression? Or was it just what it looked like, an intense spiritual experience that had broken through the routine of the correctional officer's job? To this day, I do not know.

The officer, whose name I do not remember, was not able to tell me anything about his experience, because he was still so caught up in it. I knew nothing about his life situation. All he could do was praise God. Eventually, he was able to respond to the prison administrators about what should happen with his job. They wanted him to quit, and he agreed to do so. I felt some concern about whether he should be making such a decision in his present state, but I did not try to intervene. I knew that after an incident like this, he would never be allowed to work as a correctional officer again, but I still wonder if I should have said something. I wonder about his life after this incident. Was this a spiritual experience that transformed his life, or was it just an aberration that faded into his memory as he went back to more mundane concerns? Was it an experience he regretted as a "breakdown" and a sign of weakness? Or was it the beginning of a mental illness that would profoundly affect his life in another direction? Twenty-two years later, I still do not know.

But I am confident that whatever the underlying reasons for this correctional officer's experience, that in his life, this was a real opportunity for transformation. Whether precipitated by the isolation, some other life stress, or even a biochemical process, he had encountered a most profound and awesome aspect of himself, and something beyond himself. He had touched the face of God and therefore had the opportunity for transformation into a new being, with a new life path, and with his footsteps ordered by the Almighty.

three

FAITH AND PSYCHOLOGY

> *"It is not an exaggeration to say that today man experiences his present situation in terms of disruption, conflict, self-destruction, meaninglessness, and despair in all realms of life. . . . It [the Christian message of 'New Being'] is based on what Paul calls the 'new creation' and refers to its power of overcoming the demonic cleavages of the 'old reality' in soul, society, and universe."*
>
> — PAUL TILLICH[1]

> *". . . to the extent that all mystical or peak experiences are the same in their essence and have always been the same, all religions are the same in their essence and always have been the same. They should, therefore, come to agree in principle on teaching that which is common to all of them, i.e., whatever it is that peak experiences teach in common (whatever is* different *about these illuminations can fairly be taken to be localisms both in time and space, and are, therefore, peripheral, expendable, not essential)."*
>
> — ABRAHAM MASLOW[2]

Faith and Psychology

The concept of self-actualization in psychology means to become fully and genuinely oneself, and in doing so, to achieve one's full potential. Self-actualization requires overcoming the alienation, conflict, and self-destructiveness that seem so inherent in the lives of many people. This is apparent in the rates of divorce and single-parent households, alcoholism and other addictions, homicides, depression and suicides, delinquency and school failure among children, among other ills. Psychology and its related disciplines, in their applied form of various therapies, attempt to alleviate these problems, primarily with the goal of getting the person or family to an improved level of functioning in society. Though psychology developed the concept of self-actualization, that is not its goal. The goal of self-actualization is left to religion, whether of the traditional or "new age" variety.

Scott Peck, in *The Road Less Traveled and Beyond*, has pointed out the limitations of the concept of self-actualization, stating, "I do not believe that we can actualize ourselves anymore than we can create ourselves."[3] A relationship with God, or some "center of value and power," is necessary for us as human beings to realize our true selves. Theologian James Fowler writes of the triadic covenant relationship among self, others, and a mutual "center of value and power."[3] If we do not worship God, we will deify ourselves, another person, money, power, or some other object or principle. We seem to be made in such a way that we have to invest that spiritual and psychological energy in something or someone.

Using scans and other medical instruments to examine the changes in the brain that occur during prayer and meditation, neuroscientist Andrew Newberg and colleagues concluded: "From the neurobiological perspective, human ritual has two major characteristics. First, it generates emotional discharges, in varying degrees of intensity, that represent subjective feelings of tranquility, ecstasy, and awe; and second, it results in unitary states that, in a religious context, are often experienced as some degree of spiritual transcendence."[6]

Newberg, Eugene D'Aquili, and Vince Rause speculate that based on their findings, and on the near universality of religious practice, that our neural circuits are wired for spirituality, probably because it served some evolutionary purpose. Perhaps it helped to reduce anxiety about the unknowable, enabling early humans to survive and cope in a world full of uncertainty and danger. Newberg and his colleagues further state: "It seems that more than mere autonomic stimulation is required to trigger the emotional states associated with ritual; ideas that have a deeper psychological charge or emotional pull are also required."[5] They conclude: "As long as our brains are capable of sensing this deeper reality, spirituality will continue to shape the human experience, and God, however we define that majestic, mysterious concept, will not go away."[7]

Research on what Newberg calls "neurotheology" cannot address the question of the reality of the content of spiritual experience and God, compared to the reality of material existence. That remains a matter of faith. Theologian and philosopher Paul Tillich said that "Theology has no right and no obligation to prejudice a physical or historical, sociological or psychological, inquiry. And no result of such an inquiry can be directly productive or disastrous for theology."[8] But this type of research and discussion can help some people to accept and develop their own spiritual inclinations, which they might otherwise attempt to stifle when they see it as purely irrational and archaic behavior.

Psychology can also help to clarify the function of spirituality in a healthy personality. In *New Seeds of Contemplation*, Thomas Merton discusses the Greek conception of a person as consisting of: the anima or psyche, which represents instinct and emotion; the animus, which is intelligence and reason; and the spiritus or pneuma, which is the spirit.[9] Merton states that the "spiritual life" consists not of renouncing one or the other aspects of the person, but of attaining a balance in which the instinct, emotion, and intellect operate under the guidance of the spirit, which is directed by the love of God and the Holy Spirit. I find it interesting that Sigmund Freud retained this three-part conception of human personality, but replaced the spirit with the "superego" or conscience, creating a totally naturalistic concept of the person, with no connection to God. The conscience for Freud is an internalization of the prohibitions of our individual fathers. Freud's goal for humanity was not transcendence, but a balance, or homeostasis, attained through adaptation of internal primitive impulses to the requirements of society and the physical world.

On the contrary, Merton states that it is the desires and motivations of the "false self," the self alienated from God, that causes humanity so much grief. "Our true self is, then, the self that receives freely and gladly the missions that are God's supreme gift to His sons. Any other 'self' is an illusion."[10] This goes back to my earlier statement that we have the need to worship something, if not God, then ourselves, another person, or some thing, whether material, intellectual, or emotional. Neurotheology helps explain why we have this inclination. Psychology can help clarify some aspects of the experience of faith.

For example, the fifth century North African theologian and bishop Augustine of Hippa documented in his book *The Confessions of St. Augustine* the role of habit in the perpetuation of sinful behavior, even against the person's will.[11] In this context, sin is thought, speech, or action that disrupts one's relationship with God. In a later section, I will talk further about the role of spiritual practice in breaking down habits of addiction, and of sin. Most of us are more like St. Augustine than like the apostle Paul. Paul was converted in a vision and a blinding flash of light. Even after an ecstatic mountaintop spiritual experience, most of us still struggle daily with habits that separate us from God.

At this point in the history of psychology, some of Freud's ideas are considered somewhat antiquated. Cognitive behavioral psychology, which focuses on understanding and changing behavior by focusing on expressed thoughts, emotions, and actions, is more compatible with the quantitative research orientation of modern psychology. Current behavioral scientists are primarily concerned with what is measurable and directly observable in human beings. They explain very well how habits and preferences can develop and change. However, Freud and his intellectual descendants such as Karl Jung and Erik Erikson still give a useful, if impressionistic, picture of the dynamics of how we experience ourselves and our relationships with others. The third major theoretical approach in psychology is humanistic psychology. And it is here that the concept of self-actualization developed.

Humanistic psychology is the theoretical orientation that directly acknowledges spiritual needs as essential to being human. My first encounter with humanistic psychology came when I was a student for one year in a graduate program in music therapy at Lesley College. This was just prior to beginning a graduate psychology program at Boston University. At Lesley, I saw a film showing psychologists Carl Rogers, Albert Ellis, and Karl Jung consecutively interviewing the same female patient. In this teaching film, Rogers represented the humanistic psychology, Ellis represented cognitive behavioral psychology, and Jung represented Freudian psychology. I was interested enough in Rogers to read his book *On Becoming a Person*. I believe it was also during that time or a bit later that I read *Man's Search for Meaning* by Victor Frankle. I was definitely attracted to the concepts of authenticity and the need for a spiritual life, or some other profound sense of meaning.

These ideas of humanistic psychology had been investigated and developed much more thoroughly and systematically by

Abraham Maslow. Maslow's background and training was in traditional experimental psychology (primarily using rats and other animals) as well as in Freudian psychoanalytic psychology. He had reviewed and critiqued psychoanalytic (Freudian) and behavioral schools, with the goal of integrating them into a third force, humanistic psychology. The primary concepts of Maslow's approach are "self-actualization" and the "hierarchy of needs," which evolved from his study of instincts in animals and instinct-like needs in human beings.[12] The hierarchy of needs are ordered from the physiological (such as for food and water), to safety needs, to love needs, to self-esteem needs, and at the top, the need for self-actualization or the full realizations of one's potential. Part of self-actualization involves mystical or "peak" experiences in which one transcends the everyday experience of the self.

During the 1960s and 1970s, there was an explosion of "new age" quests for peak experiences. The encounter group and other types of expressive "new age" self-improvement approaches became widespread fads. This led to excesses, with attempts to induce peak experiences as though they are just another form of intoxicant. Maslow was quite critical of these excesses, but in the mind of some people, his name became associated with this movement that was ultimately seen as superficial and destructive.

My own experiences at Lesley College definitely made me tired of the endless group expressiveness and sharing, and the lack of intellectual rigor. After that, I was happy to dig into the more intellectual or technical challenge approaches of psychoanalytic and behavioral psychology. But I did not find satisfaction there, even in graduate school and clinical internship. Trained in the clinician-scientist-teacher model of psychology, my professional work began with direct clinical work in hospital, clinic, and correctional settings and then shifted to founding and managing business organizations in the mental health and health care consulting fields. As I reached age fifty, it became more essential for me to place all my experiences into an integrated perspective, in order to more fully come to terms with my life, and to distill something from that experience that might be of value to others.

When I started a company to provide billing services and online access to practice management software for mental health service providers in mid-2000, I decided on the name Actualize, Inc. In doing so, I was consciously referring to psychologist Abraham Maslow's concept of self-actualization: that once the more basic physiological, safety, love, and esteem needs are met, people seek to become fully what they are potentially.

I was aware that for at least a year or two, I had been feeling this intensified urgency and had been having an internal dialogue about more fully understanding what my life was about. I had been thinking about this more in terms of Erik Erikson's stages of life and had not considered Abraham Maslow's ideas prior to naming the company. Things came to a head one day as I sat at my desk feeling a mixture of frustration and urgency. It occurred to me that I needed to devote more time to writing and studying as a way of making sense of my experiences. In that same moment it was clear to me that self-actualization would be the organizing concept for me in accomplishing this task. I also realized that I had never looked seriously into self-actualization and Abraham Maslow. I immediately did an Internet search on him and got a list of his work. Then and there I ordered his books, his biography, and the taped interview done by Warren Bennis. In reading Maslow, I felt that I had found the missing link to understanding my own experiences across clinical psychology, academic psychology, and business.

But my midlife search for self-understanding and peace did not find resolution in humanistic psychology. I had been attending church regularly since 1997, and I had begun to relate my own struggles more and more in biblical terms. I had begun keeping a journal in December 2000. From December to March, my journal entries discussed issues in psychological, philosophical, and business terms. Then abruptly on March 22, 2001, I made a journal entry titled "Faith in Adversity."

In that journal entry, I talked about a business setback. A deal to purchase another small company seemed to have fallen apart that day. This development pushed me to face the prospect of letting this dream go. I surmised that perhaps the greatest challenge of a setback is not the objective event itself but the way it affects one's internal balance. Or that perhaps even more profoundly, the two are inseparable. I wrote that I needed to pull back and regain my equilibrium in order to find the correct solution or path through the confused and difficult situation. Then my thoughts turned to the Bible. I thought that I understood then something about the biblical book of Job.

I wrote: "One must maintain faith and avoid bitterness and despair even in the midst of suffering and setbacks. Of course, what I'm dealing with is nothing compared to physical suffering and the death of loved ones. But most of us do deal with the loss of loved ones and manage to still find the optimism and faith to go on living. But there is a process of grieving followed by adjustment. This includes periods of depression and temporary loss of the desire for life. According to the Bible, even Jesus had moments of doubt, when faced with the reality of impending arrest and death, and expressed feelings of being forsaken by God when dying on the cross. Then later, he came to terms with it and died at peace. Now these situations may seem totally unrelated to a potentially derailed business deal, but I think that a similar principle is at work. I had become so invested in this acquisition as a way of securing my livelihood and my professional identity that the prospect of its failure gave me a small taste of fear and psychological death. Whether in Christianity or Zen Buddhism, the spiritual stance does require that I let go of my ego-driven hold on life and live it in a less fearful and self-oriented way. In doing so, I can live more fully and authentically. This is the path I committed myself to thirty-one years ago when I dropped out of Harvard University. And it is the only path that is real and true for me. I still have a lot of growing to do."

Something had changed in my frame of reference. From that day forward, my journal entries reflect an increasing focus on biblical concepts. My life also changed. Instead of just attending church, I became more actively involved. I joined the health ministry and attended Bible study. At home, I began a daily program of reading Scripture and praying several times a day. Always an avid reader, I continued my informal research of topics of interest to me, but now my focus shifted to theology and the history of Christianity.

Faith began working for me for two reasons. I found it helpful to relate my own struggles to those of other human beings over the 3,500-year history recorded in the Bible. I also began to experience directly the effects of connecting with God's Holy Spirit. As I prayed, my thinking and feelings changed. I began to let go and to realize that there was another way to be, that by letting go, my thoughts, words, and actions became ordered by the living principle of the Holy Spirit. Instead of worry and anxiety, I could experience peace and joy. I wept frequently at church, tears of joy and gratitude that God was enabling me to become whole. My relationship with my wife Glenda was strengthened, as we found a common profound principle to organize our lives together. We were also able to provide better leadership and support for our daughter, daughter-in-law, and their four children, all of whom lived with us for a time. After they moved to their own apartments, church activities for both the adults and the children continued to help structure our weekly life.

As I further studied the Bible, the history of Christianity, and the works of theologians, I continually grew in understanding of the meaning of words that I had read and sung all my life. I learned that it is important to understand the doctrines of my faith tradition, Christian Protestant theology, and to wherever possible, to be able to join in affirmation, saying "Amen." But I also learned that more important to me than doctrine, is the transformation of my being and my life through a direct relationship with the Holy Spirit, cultivated through prayer, study, and practice.

In *Dynamics of Faith*, theologian Paul Tillich says, "Faith is not an act of any of his rational functions, as it is not an act of the unconscious, but it is an act in which both the rational and nonrational elements of his being are transcended."[13] As I discussed earlier, the classical Greek conception of a person consisted of: the anima or psyche, which represents instinct and emotion; the animus, which is intelligence and reason; and the spiritus or pneuma, which is the spirit. Psychology deals with the psyche (emotion and instinct) and animus (intellect). Religion deals with the spirit. Merton states that the "spiritual life" consists not of renouncing one or the other aspects of the person, but of attaining a balance in which the instinct, emotion, and intellect operate under the guidance of the spirit, which is directed by the love of God and the Holy Spirit.

Transformation into a new being involves more than self-actualization. Becoming fully and authentically oneself, requires both psychology and faith. It takes faith and spiritual discipline to connect with the transforming power of God's Holy Spirit. "Do not conform any longer to the pattern of this world, but be transformed by the renewing of your mind. Then you will be able to test and approve what God's will is—his good, pleasing, and perfect will."[14] And psychology can help change the habitual behaviors that separate us from God, and cause so much misery to ourselves and others.

Addiction and Sin

> *"For they mouth empty, boastful words and, by appealing to the lustful desires of sinful human nature, they entice people who are just escaping from those who live in error. They promise them freedom, while they themselves are slaves of depravity—for a man is a slave to whatever has mastered him."*
>
> — 2 PETER 2:18-19[15]

Archbishop Fulton Sheen, author of *A Life is Worth Living*, argued against the disease concept of alcoholism. He thought that the Christian concept of it as slavery is better, because slavery indicates the possibility of freedom of will and responsibility (as least at some points in the addiction process).[16] He also talked about people drinking not so much because they like to drink, as because they cannot cope with life's shocks. Psychologists and others in the helping profession probably like the disease concept of addiction because it avoids blaming the addicted person. While it is worthwhile, both psychologically and spiritually, to avoid condemning people, it may be that by removing the element of responsibility, we make it more difficult for a person to recover.

Similarly, many people today probably find the concept of sin too narrowly moralistic and judgmental. But sin is actually a very democratic concept in an accurate reading of the Bible. "For we have all sinned, and come short of the Glory of God." Sin is not a pejorative that you throw at someone else, rather it is a humble recognition of the condition with which we all struggle. Alcoholics Anonymous and similar programs expect that each person say, "Hello, my name is __, and I am an alcoholic." Similarly, for each of us to become reconciled with God, which is the only way to become fully who we are, we must each eschew our shame and state, "Hello, my name is __, and I am a sinner." Moral condescension disappears with the realization that, like addiction, we cannot avoid sin through exercising will power. We must call upon a higher power, and rely upon the community of believers for support in maintaining our recovery.

Habit is an important part of forming an addiction. There is surely variation in the biological vulnerability to addiction. And certainly there is a biochemical mechanism underlying the addiction process. But a behavior like gambling, which does not involve introducing a chemical substance into the body, can become addictive. That addiction can become totally absorbing, so that the person pursues the activity to the extent of social self-destruction and the destruction of familial relationships. This indicates that habit is probably more powerful than physical dependence in the mechanism of addiction. Overcoming physical dependence in alcohol and other drug addiction does require facing the pain and sickness of withdrawal and detoxification. But this is not the primary obstacle to ending the addiction.

The primary problem is the tendency to relapse. This is not a problem of physical dependence. It is a psychological and spiritual problem. Of course, one can have a craving for a drug, whether it is nicotine or alcohol, but the person will not die if he does not have a cigarette or a drink. He relapses because he has not found the motivation and support to develop alternative ways of dealing with the anxiety he experiences when he doesn't smoke or drink. It is that anxiety that is the root problem. We all experience anxiety, some more than others. Some of this is based on the differences in the circuitry of our nervous systems, and some of it is based on differences in individual life experience.

Usually, will power is not enough to prevent relapse in addiction. The most successful method (as in twelve step programs) involves participating in a group where one is encouraged to acknowledge: that one is an addict; that one is unable to use will power to end the addiction, but must surrender to a higher power (God), and live one day at a time; and that one will never be cured, but can sustain recovery through support of this alternative society.

The process of addiction is similar to the process of sin. St. Augustine describes sin this way: "I asked, 'What is iniquity?' and I found that it is not a substance. It is perversity of will, twisted away from the supreme substance, yourself, O God, and toward lower things, and casting away its own bowels, and swelling beyond itself."[17] Sin is when one's spirit is captured by something other than God. It can be an object or person that is desirable or beautiful. It can be oneself, where we puff ourselves up in our own eyes and the eyes of others. The other side to these sins of desire and pride are fear, envy, and hatred. We respond with these when we perceive the object of desire, including our self-image, to be threatened. Sometimes the threat is obvious, while at other times, we just feel anxious for no apparent reason.

This existential anxiety seems to be just part and parcel of who we are as human beings. All our material needs may be met, and we may be surrounded by loving family and friends, but at any moment, for no particular reason, we can experience that momentary sense of fear and insecurity. But this is not really irrational. So much of life is beyond our control. We are subject to accidents, economic decline, illness, early death, and if we live long enough, old age and inevitable death. Nothing we can do can bring these factors under control. So we grab onto things, people, and activities that divert our attention from this anxiety.

We are all predisposed to sin, that is, to putting ourselves, things, and people in the place of God. It can be as minor as a passing thought or desire, or as gross as murder. "We have all sinned and fallen short of the glory of God." And we do it every day. Is it habit, that is, learned behavior, or is it part of our basic biological makeup to resort to fear, selfishness, hatred, and envy on the slightest provocation, or without any provocation? Or is a combination of habit and nature?

Reading the Old Testament, it is clear that people, even God's people, have been caught in that cycle of sin, punishment, redemption, and sin again for thousands of years. And today, some of us go through that cycle every day, or even several times a day. We may not be sleeping with another man's wife, and then arranging for the man's death like King David did; but by thought, word, or deed, we separate ourselves from God and attach ourselves to things and people in ways that violate our relationship with God. In doing so, we violate our own spirit and our spiritual relationship with others.

For Christians, Jesus' sacrifice of himself offers us salvation that we could not obtain by our own efforts to conform to the law of the Old Testament. We are saved from the penalty of sin, but not from the process of recurrent sin. We acknowledge our inability to free ourselves of sin and accept salvation through grace. We will sin despite all our efforts, but by dedicating our lives to God through prayer, study, and practice, we align our will with God's will and experience lasting spiritual peace and joy here on earth.

This does not mean that we must all turn away from the physical and social world and live only for a spiritual paradise that comes after death. It is easy to understand some Scripture in that manner: "Do not love the world or anything in the world. If anyone loves the world, the love of the Father is not in him. For everything in the world—the cravings of sinful man, the lusts of the eyes and boastings of what he has and does—comes not from the Father but from the world."[18] St. Augustine helps clarify this: "If you find pleasure in bodily things, praise God for them, and direct your love to their maker, lest because of things that please you, you may displease him. If you find pleasure in souls, let them be loved in God. In themselves they are but shifting things; in him they stand firm; else they would pass and perish."[19]

Loving the things of the world is not sin. Sin is loving those things in place of, or above, God, rather than loving them through God. We sin when we think, speak, or act not out of the love of God, but out of selfish motivation such as pride, fear, anger, greed, and envy. Two thousand years ago, the first Christians lived in expectation of the imminent return of Christ and the end of the physical world, while enduring persecution for their faith, which was considered an illegal cult. It is understandable that for them, the kingdom of God was to be found someplace other than in this world, and life on earth was not valued. But Jesus described it differently. Once, having been asked by the Pharisees when the kingdom of God would come, Jesus replied, "The kingdom of God does not come with your careful observation, nor will people say, 'Here it is', or 'There it is', because the kingdom of God is within you [or among you]."[20] And in the Lord's Prayer, Jesus said:

> Your kingdom come.
> Your will be done
> On earth as it is in heaven.
> — Luke 11:2[21]

The central Christian message is the transformation of each believer by salvation through Jesus Christ. "Do not conform any longer to the pattern of this world, but be transformed by the renewing of your mind. Then you will be able to test and approve what God's will is—his good, pleasing, and perfect will."[22] Each person is transformed through a personal relationship with God's Holy Spirit, made possible by the sacrifice of Jesus Christ. Jesus said to his disciples that he must leave this world so that the Holy Spirit may come to empower each of them. And they in turn could carry the message of salvation to all the world. "Now I am going to him who sent me, yet none of you asks me, 'Where are you going?' Because I have said these things, you are filled with grief. But I tell you the truth: It is for your good that I am going away. Unless I go away, the Counselor will not come to you; but if I go, I will send him to you."[23]

I believe that what Christians experience as the Holy Spirit is experienced by people of other faiths under other names and concepts. When I first experienced it at age nineteen, I interpreted it in the vague quasi-Buddhist framework used by the 1960s subculture of which I was part. But it was an experience disembodied from most of the previous nineteen years of my life. Today, the stories, songs, and rituals of Christianity give depth to all the experiences of my particular life. But I can readily understand how another system of meaning, with its stories, symbols, and rituals, can give immediacy and depth to someone else's experience of God.

It is through the power of the Holy Spirit that a believer is renewed and enabled to maintain the discipline to each day conform his thinking words and actions to the will of God. The community of the church is a twelve step program of sorts, in which one must confess: "I am a sinner, and I do not have the power to save myself from sin. I can only humble myself before God, and ask for his help in transforming my life." The fellowship of the church community helps to support and reinforce the new behaviors that break the habits of a sinful past. But this will only work if the discipline of prayer and study of the Bible becomes part of one's daily life; not as a dry ritual, but as a living and refreshing relationship with God's Holy Spirit, which is within each of us.

> Each day, we must cry out:
> "Create in me a pure heart, O God,
> and renew a steadfast spirit within me.
> Do not cast me from your presence
> or take your Holy Spirit from me.
> Restore to me the joy of your salvation
> and grant me a willing spirit, to sustain me."
> — Psalm 51:10-12[24]

Lord, create in me a pure heart and a renewed mind. For the mind and heart to become clean, habits of thought, speech, and action must be purified. Through association and conditioning, the new habits consistent with the Love of God take the place of old habits. But this is not just a process of brainwashing through repetition (though that works to some extent in changing behavior, as the behavioral and cognitive behavioral psychologists have shown). There must also be a working through, a coming to terms with, and resolving of deep conflicts and negative impulses that power the old habits. (In that sense, Freud was right.) True transformation must involve intellectual understanding, emotional cleansing or catharsis, and practice of new behaviors. By intellectual understanding, I mean that the Scriptures (the words and symbols of a people's historical relationship with God) must make sense in light of our actual experiences (intellectual, moral, emotional, and physical).

"Consequently, faith comes from hearing the message, and the message is heard through the word of Christ."[25] Developing a personal relationship with God through understanding his word, and the mediation of Jesus Christ and the Holy Spirit, must become a genuine, holistic experience. It is clear that the Scriptures have not changed for almost two thousand years. But our understanding of the words must be something that grows and develops (as our lives and situations change over the centuries) in order for it to remain alive and directly relevant to our lives today.

Therefore, each of us must, in his or her own way but in a way that joins us with the past and present, seek to directly apprehend the words and symbols of our particular faith traditions. Of course, over the centuries, the original Christian church has split into denominations as a result of differing interpretations of the word, and resulting differences in practice. Wars have been fought and heretics burned over these differences. But time does make the final determination. Ultimately, the interpretations that survive are the ones that people need to help make sense and meaning of their lives.

Our clerics and preachers should be the most advanced in understanding and interpreting the Christian gospel, because it is their profession, and their time is primarily dedicated to that and to ministering to the needs of their church members and others. But I expect that the institutional and cultural constraints of their positions might sometimes keep them from being in the vanguard, and make them tend to be more conservative. Conserving is essential, but someone must also create new paths, though this may risk being condemned by the established church. The important thing is for each person to seek to genuinely know God, in the sense of having a personal relationship through prayer, study, practice, and helping others along the way.

Power and Powerlessness

> *"Power, properly understood, is the ability to achieve purpose. It is the strength required to bring about social, political, or economic changes. In this sense, power is not only desirable but necessary in order to implement the demands of love and justice. . . . What is needed is a realization that power without love is reckless and abusive and that love without power is sentimental and anemic. Power at its best is love implementing the demands of justice. Justice at its best is love correcting everything that stands against love."*
> — MARTIN LUTHER KING JR.[26]

> *"Growth requires connection and trust. Alienation is a form of living death. It is the acid of despair that dissolves society."*
> — MARTIN LUTHER KING JR.[27]

Powerlessness, meaninglessness, normlessness, isolation, and self-estrangement were discussed by sociologists studying criminal behavior in the 1950s as being elements of alienation.[28] Based on this work of sociologists, psychologists have developed means of measuring powerlessness, using standardized questionnaires. The most widely used measure of powerlessness is Rotter's Internal-External (I-E) Control Scale.[29] This is powerlessness as perceived by the person himself or herself, which may or may not be related to his or her "objective" situation as observed by someone else. In this model, a person feels powerful when he or she perceives that the achievement of desired goals lies within his or her own capabilities and, thus, would score higher on the internal end of the I-E scale. By contrast, people who believe that the achievement of desired goals were primarily dependent on something other than themselves would experience themselves as powerless, and rate higher on the external end of the I-E scale.

This idea of powerlessness has been found to be particularly effective in understanding clinical depression. In that context, powerlessness has been conceptualized as "learned helplessness." Simply put, people become depressed in part because they learn that any attempt on their part to improve their situation is futile. Psychologist Martin Seligman's experiment that induced learning helpfulness in dogs through electric shock made a great impact on our understanding of depression. This would lead him to develop a "positive psychology" based on the idea that positive attitudes (happiness) can be learned, just like depression.[30]

Seligman and others have done the empirical research for a theory of positive psychology, which focuses on understanding the healthy as opposed to the pathological in human beings. Humanistic psychologists, especially Abraham Maslow, have traditionally been the ones who did this, while others focused on psychopathology and deviant behavior. However, humanistic psychologists also talk about ideas like self-actualization, which ultimately lead to discussion of spirituality and mystical experiences. The positive psychologists want to talk about the "positive" rather than about the "good" or about "God." So they have distanced themselves from the humanistic psychologists.

Perhaps they chose the word "positive" because it sounds more scientific, like positive and negative charges in physics. Or perhaps it indicates their subscription to the theory of positivism, which holds that theology and metaphysics have been made obsolete by empirical science.

By operationalizing the concept of powerlessness as learned helplessness, and eliminating anything with the taint of spirituality, the positive psychologists are doing something similar to what Freud did when he secularized the Greek schema of the personality by changing spiritus (spirit) into the concept of superego (conscience). This limits the field of activity to phenomena that are more readily observable and measurable. Much good can be accomplished by this, in terms of the development and application of the scientific methods to understanding human beings and alleviating suffering. But as Tillich states, "The banishment of religion into the nonrational corner of subjective emotions in order to have the realms of thought and action free from religious interference was an easy way of escaping the conflicts between religious tradition and modern thought. But this was a death sentence against religion, and religion did not and could not accept it."[31]

More than a death sentence for religion, it is a death sentence for a fractured and alienated humanity. The psychological research on power and powerlessness would lead one to believe that the solution to happiness is to learn to perceive oneself as having more power, the opposite of learned helplessness. But the reality is more complex than that. For example, the positive psychology researchers have found that poverty makes people unhappy, but that once people reach a level of reasonable comfort, wealth does not add up to happiness. There is no more profound explanation of this than Maslow's hierarchy of needs, which states that once basic needs are somewhat satisfied, higher and ultimately spiritual needs become of predominant concern.

Even the concept of internal versus external control has deeper implications, and the issue becomes not simply a choice between power and powerlessness. There is also a choice between demonic power and the power of God. Demonic power becomes evident when an alienated being, separated from God, attributes to himself or some other object, the power that actually belongs to God. The extreme example may be a megalomaniac like Hitler, but an ordinary example may be simple misplaced pride that leads to actions and consequences. Power that is not accompanied by humility and love becomes demonic. As soon as one attributes power to oneself, humility disappears and the ego becomes inflated. If one attributes power to someone or something else, love and humility are replaced by fear, envy, and hatred.

Without God, the choice is between being powerless or being demonic. With God, one can be powerful, humble, and loving. This is because the power is not ours; we are not using it for our own selfish desires. We first assume a humble position and submit ourselves and our lives to the will of God. Then we become empowered through the Holy Spirit working in our personality and our lives. We become transformed into new beings. Psyche, which represents instinct and emotion, and the animus, which is intelligence and reason, are unified under the guidance of the spirit. The power is not possessed by us, for that would be demonic. Rather it is a power that resides in us. It is not ours, but we are made more than we are through our connection with it. This confounds the distinction of internal versus external control.

Machiavellianism is the closest concept to demonic power that I have seen in psychology. It justifies the use of force and deceit to accumulate power for oneself, without regard to right or wrong, good or evil.[32] It justifies this behavior by attributing the same heartless motives to everyone else. Its mantra becomes, "Do it to others, before they do it to you."

But the very fact that the Machiavellian person needs to justify his own selfishness by attributing the same motive to others, suggests that he knows, perhaps subconsciously, that what he is doing is wrong. Freud's idea of the psychological defense he called projection, is still valid today, as it was in biblical times. It is far easier to see the mote in another's eye, than the beam, in one's own eye; and the evil we see in others justifies our own evil actions.

Paradoxically, compared with the learned helplessness idea of positive psychology, in Christ we become powerful by acknowledging our ultimate helplessness before God. This enables us to act powerfully, not as an ego-inflated demonic self, but as our true self united with God in humility and love.

four

MUSIC AND REVELATION

"If you would know the real life and history of a nation or a people, study the testimony it makes in its songs. . . . When life runs over, it is expressed in song. When the heart is too full of sorrow or joy for speech, it sings. This makes song one of the most precious forms of the practice of testimony."
— THOMAS HOYT JR.[1]

Music at its core is tied to revelation; for it has no true purpose but to praise God, and in doing so, to edify humankind. Like all the works of human beings, it can be used to degrade the spirit, but that is not its true purpose. I am not speaking just about gospel or other overtly religious music, or even just music with words. I mean any music that opens the ears and the heart. Because if it does this, even without intending to, it touches the spirit. It may be intended only to be a love song, but as long as it does not become demonic, and actively negates and degrades the human spirit, it will become a song in praise of God or creation, or a song expressing longing for communion with him. For God is the source of love and of creativity, and music is a system of human communication and praise of God based on sound, silence, and time; more specifically rhythm, melody, harmony, and lyrics.

The music may be played as written from the page, performed

from memory exactly as taught, or improvised orally based on a song. It can be a simple melody, a rhythm, or some combination of these. The form of the music and the technique applied by the musicians are important and must conform to the particular cultural context; but at some point, to be effective, it must transcend these and create a situation where time stops, and both the performers and audience become engaged in the music as an authentic communal enterprise.

There is a point at which language, which is our primary communication tool, fails to express the depths of our spirit and experience. That's when we turn to music (and the other arts). The music may include words, but the words are not merely technical tools for the business of everyday life. The words themselves contain music, as in poetry, where their sounds and meanings play their own form of melody, harmony, and rhythm. In using words or sounds thus, we joyfully or sorrowfully recognize there is more to "meaning" than rational sense-making and more to "purpose" than "objective." We come to understand that as spiritual beings, we hunger for something more than material sustenance: "Man does not live on bread alone but on every word that comes from the mouth of the Lord."[2] The words that come from the mouth of God are not likely to be functional business English for writing memos and objectives, though those also have their place. Rather, they are words whose meanings we may not grasp logically, but which instead catch us up in an ecstatic dance, where time stands still, and each moment is full of significance; and which also have the power to transform our personalities and our communities.

In the MCI Arena in Washington DC, a huge indoor stadium built for basketball and hockey, the music was so clear and pure on a particular night, that it was as if it were played on acoustic instruments. Every instrument could be heard clearly, and in the silence between phrases, you could hear a pin drop. And the emotions portrayed by the sung lyrics, the voices, the instruments, and the light show were so real and true, that it seemed as though you could touch them, or rather that the singer, musicians, and light show artists played directly on your heart rather than on their instruments. This was a Luther Vandross concert, and the content was romantic love songs. As I sat with my wife Glenda, I had fleeting thoughts about the relationship between romantic love and the love of God. I also thought about the relationship between technical excellence and authentic expression in musical performance. In the highest art, the spiritual subsumes the esthetic, providing a new direction and point of resolution for its skills and striving.

A member of my church once said something to this effect, "I don't really care if someone can sing well, as long as they sing from the heart and consistent with the Holy Spirit." Others present in the meeting agreed. I remained silent. I had been thinking about this very issue of whether technical excellence is important in the spiritual realm, as it is in the esthetic, and had not yet reached clarity about it. There certainly is a difference between the two worlds. In the context of a prayer and worship service, a singer who is touched by the Holy Spirit but who has severely limited musical skills can be more effective than a singer with great technique, who clearly lacks the conviction of the Holy Spirit. However, when technical excellence and conviction comes together, oh, what a great blessing that is. It truly can increase the intensity and depth of the assembled body's experience of the Holy Spirit. So both is better, but if a choice is necessary, a sincere worshipper must choose the Holy Spirit.

Now in esthetic music, or art music, which is performed in a concert hall, jazz club, or other secular gathering place, and which involves a tradition of highly developed technique, the situation differs considerably. Probably jazz and European classical music are the two most highly developed and global forms. In both jazz and classical music, the audience responds most enthusiastically when virtuoso performance is combined with profound emotional and conceptual meaning. Time stands still, and we are caught up in the rhythmic, melodic, and harmonic story, with its compelling emotions and characters.

In the esthetic world, technically excellent but sterile and meaningless music is probably more acceptable than it is in the spiritual sphere. Conversely, in the esthetic world, poor technique is unforgivable. This is more so in classical music, where the musicians are reproducing a composer's written work. In jazz, advanced technique is also highly valued, but the great musician is not expected to repeat the notes he or she has practiced. He or she is expected to push pass this known territory in order to express and create something new. Therefore "wrong" notes in John Coltrane's or Miles Davis's solos serve an expressive purpose, even when they are not intentional. They become part of what is being created and lead to something new being expressed. A related example is Ella Fitzgerald's version of "Mack the Knife." She forgot the lyrics and invented new ones that made fun of her own forgetfulness, and then transcended it to create an exciting improvised event. Would we really prefer that she had sung the lyrics perfectly the way they were written, and completed the song without incident or danger or such remarkable creativity?

The relationship between technical excellence and authenticity is also important in everyday life. Technical excellence without genuineness can become intellectual obsession, or it can become physical or emotional behavior patterns that we have practiced for so long that they are performed without much attention or involvement. The word "authenticity" does not convey the full meaning intended, because more than emotional sincerity, what's also involved is a resonance that emanates from the content of what is communicated, as well as from the materials with which it is communicated. This creates layers of meaning beyond that of which even the person communicating is aware. It touches and stimulates the mind and conscious emotions and then goes beyond them to something infinite and universal—to spirit.

Musical Pictures from Life's Exhibition

Sounds from Childhood

I do not remember lullabies or many children's songs from childhood. But when it started raining while we were in class at Mr. Pete's one-room schoolhouse, the solid wooden windows had to be closed. Without outside light, we could do no work. So our teacher led us in songs like "Row, row, row your boat," to while away the time until the rain stopped. At such times, singing together, snugly closed up in the large single room, with the rain pounding on the outside, felt a little like being in Noah's ark; as if we were the only living people left on the face of the earth. The gratification and stress of competition for our teacher's attention and best grades were temporarily forgotten. We were no longer one against the other, racing for the goal, but all together as one.

At home, I remember staying within earshot of my mother as she sang and went about her housework. One song that particularly touched me was "Tennessee Waltz," a song of lost love and betrayal by a best friend. As my mother sang it, it seemed inexplicably beautiful and sad. I did not understand the difference between the sacred and the secular, and that song was just as profound, though not as spectacular, to me at that time as the singing of Handel's Hallelujah Chorus by the Moravian Church choir on Easter. The song that my mother sang was sad, but she did not seem sad. Rather, I sensed her joy in the act of singing. And it was perhaps that mixture of her joy in singing and the sad content of the song's story that touched and moved me in a mysterious way.

Music during worship service at the Moravian Church was more centered on spectacle than on physical or emotional participation. The massive church organ was located up in the rear balcony, facing the pulpit, which also was on its own small balcony, raised well above the heads of the worshippers seated on the first floor. For us small boys, the sound of the minister's sermon had no music in it, and nothing to hold our attention, except where a word here or there might have some humorous meaning within the context of our child's play. The word "money," for example, had a sexual meaning in our local dialect, so we would giggle every time he said it. The sermon was delivered in an emotional monotone and accepted in silence. I whiled the time away looking at the pretty stained glass windows along the side, and particularly the large one behind the minister, which displayed the Moravian emblem of a lamb carrying a flag, with the words "Our lamb has conquered. Let us follow him."

From a child's perspective, the Moravian Church came to life with the singing of the choir and the playing of the organ, particularly on special occasions such as Easter. The organ was particularly interesting because it seemed so huge, and yet it would not work unless one of the strong men pumped up and down on a large wooden handle sticking out of its left side. It seemed to me a magical beast that had to be fed with air in order to make beautiful music.

Outside of the formal worship service, the Moravian Church became more intimate and participative in activities such as the children's Christmas play and the meetings of the Boys Life troupe, which was a local version of the Boys Scout. But it was at Church of God, particularly in Sunday school, that we sang songs about God and Jesus and heard the stories of the Bible in a small group setting, which helped make religion personally and emotionally compelling.

The daily soundtrack of childhood was not church music, but the calypso songs with merengue rhythms of The Mighty Sparrow, who was in perpetual verbal competition with the other popular singer, Lord Melody. Music floated from the two rum shops at opposite corners of my street, providing a seemingly constant background to our play in the yard and street. In addition to exciting melody and rhythms, calypso songs gave us a stream of witty and insightful commentary on politics, relationships, and the human condition as perceived from Afro-Caribbean culture.

During carnival, the entire town became a stage as steel bands paraded through the streets followed by throngs of dancing people. Carnival began at dawn on Christmas day and continued until New Year's Day. Small troupes of costumed players put on dramatic-comedic displays in various neighborhoods. The mock-a-jumbee, costumed men on stilts representing ghosts, danced and amazed the small children. Clowns dressed in ballooning multicolored jumpsuits with numerous little bells jangled and pranced around, cracking their whips. Dressed in peacock-feathered headgear and with tomahawks, costumed local people formed American Indian troupes and performed their ritual dances. Later, as an adult, I wondered if this practice was a cultural memory of the Arawaks and Caribs who populated the islands prior to the arrival of the European colonizers and African slaves, and who were exterminated in the process of colonization.

But more exciting and terrifying than any other play was the bull. This was a man dressed in all red with a pair of real bull's horns attached to his head. The news would spread throughout the neighborhoods when the bull was approaching. The children were struck by a mixture of fascination and terror. The bull would chase people and pretend to gore them with his horns, as the accompanying drum and fife played dramatically.

This secular culture of calypso and carnival coexisted with church culture without any apparent contradiction. Like the blues and gospel traditions in the U.S., the musical forms cross-fertilized each other, which was not surprising since the same musicians participated in both.

The Rapture
After moving with my family to the United States at the age of

twelve, my musical soundtrack changed. Rhythm and blues music, which I had previously heard only occasionally on the radio in St. Kitts, now became my predominant soundscape. My sister Marilane, who had come to the U.S. a year before the rest of us, introduced us to the latest records and dance styles. We did not need much encouragement. What's not to love? It had exciting rhythms, touching stories of love lost and found, wonderful harmonies, and humor. I still occasionally listened to a Caribbean steel band record I had, straining to catch the world I had lost, but for the most part, rhythm and blues music felt like home.

My stepfather made his own cultural adaptation to coming to America, which focused on Nat King Cole records and the soundtrack of Broadway musicals, especially the *Sound of Music*. These struck my ear as rich and pretty, but adult stuff, nothing that I could relate to directly. But especially with Nat King Cole, this was my first introduction to jazz, a music I would eventually come to deeply appreciate. But meanwhile, rhythm and blues owned my ears; that is, until the strains of alienation and discontent in the form of the rock and folk music of the 1960s crashed into my consciousness, matching the televised news of the civil rights movement, the Vietnam War, and finally, the assassinations of Robert Kennedy and Dr. Martin Luther King Jr.

Something changed about the way I experienced music in my early twenties. Part of it was the passing away of the 1960s cultural zeitgeist, which had infused even technically mediocre music with an almost sacred meaningfulness. In that 1960s musical world, it was frequently the words that led and made the song, investing it with generational political significance, such as Bob Dylan's version of Stevie Wonder's "Blowing in the Wind," or with the mixture of romantic love and spirituality in Leonard Cohen's "Suzanne." For more purely instrumental energy and virtuosity, we had Jimi Hendrix, Eric Clapton, and the orchestrated songs of The Beatles. Spicing up that mix of mostly rock and folk was the rhythm and blues of Otis Redding and a bit of jazz from Rahsaan Roland Kirk.

It was through Rahsaan Roland Kirk that a new way of experiencing music began to infiltrate my consciousness. That the flute was one of his best instruments and that I was learning to play the flute probably helped a great deal. It was with Roland Kirk that the words started to fade into the background as the voices of the instruments themselves began speaking to my spirit. But it was Hubert Laws, the classical flutist turned jazz and Latin-jazz musician and composer extraordinaire, who blasted open the door to this new level of musical consciousness.

Sitting on the floor at a friend's apartment, listening to Laws' flute improvisation, I could not believe what I was hearing. I had now learned enough about the flute that I could not pretend not to understand its voice. The level of energy, the intensity, the depth of meaningful emotive expression, and the intellectual clarity spoke of a mastery, commitment, and rapture beyond belief.

After the experience with Hubert Laws, I no longer got much satisfaction listening to rock radio stations, so I turned to jazz and classical ones. The first day I did this, I lay in bed listening. It did not matter whether it was early Louis Armstrong and his contemporaries, or string quartets and orchestral music. It was the same experience of receiving an infusion of intense high energy, laced with the subtlest and most delicate emotions. It was a rapture.

The best singers of blues, gospel, and other folk music have always had the ability to go well beyond the words, to find an acoustic resonance that causes something deep within our spirit to vibrate sympathetically. Today, years of fertilization from jazz and classical musicians and arrangers have raised the sound quality of rhythm and blues, gospel, and Latin (salsa and merengue) recorded music to high levels of technical excellence. When the genuineness and spontaneity of the folk forms are also retained, the resulting combination approaches transcendence. This is particularly true of gospel music, where the spiritual content of the lyrics interacts with the exaltation of beautifully executed melody, harmony, and rhythm, producing a cosmic event, which can stop time, if the listener/participant responds with spirit, and not just with ears. As in all forms of revelation, revelation in music can only be experienced through the spirit.

Mobilization for Survival

In 1976, while a music student at Berklee College, I got involved with Mobilization for Survival, which organized demonstrations and teaching events against nuclear weapons and the danger of nuclear war. As a natural outgrowth of my interests, I became an informal music and performance arts leader for the Boston branch. My enthusiasm sometimes outran my political maturity, and the Boston leadership, who were sociology professors and other middle-aged and experienced activists, on one occasion had to apply a firm editorial hand to one of the songs I had written for the group.

The song was about war becoming obsolete, and the objectionable phrase was ". . . and war will be just a game that children play." They rightly objected that children should not be playing war games, and that the violent games of children socialize them into becoming potentially violent adults. What is obvious to me today was not so obvious at age twenty-six, but I understood it once it was pointed out to me.

A less controversial creation was a brief performance aimed at dramatizing the destruction of the world by nuclear weapons. In it, a male and a female danced and gestured at a dying earth projected onto a screen on the stage, accompanied by a recording of Hubert Laws playing the solo flute composition *Syrinx*, written by Claude Debussy. Laws, who played with the New York Metropolitan Opera Orchestra and the New York Philharmonic before concentrating on a career in jazz, beautifully integrated classical and Latin music into his jazz work. In this case, he overdubbed a second flute line, turning Debussy's solo composition into a haunting duet with himself. *Merriam-Webster's Dictionary* defines syrinx as "the vocal organ of birds that is a special modification of the lower part of the trachea or of the bronchi or of both." The piece is appropriately reminiscent of birds' songs and was effective for the theme of our short performance. What would the world be without the songs of birds and the music of human beings?

Gospel Songs for Billy's Mother

Billy, a mildly mentally retarded middle-aged white man, and his frail elderly mother lived together in an old house near Eggelston Station in Boston. It was a poor community that was almost exclusively African-American and Hispanic. The old house was apparently the last outpost of what was formerly a primarily white middle-class community. They were now stranded by the flux of time and circumstances. In 1978, I was a counselor in an elderly outreach program, and I visited people like Billy's mother, who were referred to us by the home health agency from the nearby Boston University Medical Center.

Billy's mother could not talk very much or very coherently, but she loved to hear me play old gospel songs on the flute. She definitely had a discriminating ear. One day I forgot my flute when I went to visit her, and I tried instead to sing some of the gospel songs for her. She made a face and started murmuring and wailing in criticism. I stopped singing and just sat with her for awhile; she was okay with that. That was the last time I went to see her without my flute.

Thinking about Billy and his mother and some of the other elderly people I visited makes me wonder about the meaning of community in post-modern society. Who values people when they no longer have market value?

five

GOD, SELF AND COMMUNITY

> "Agape *is love seeking to preserve and create community. . . .*
> Agape *is a willingness to go to any length to restore community.*
> *. . . The cross is the eternal expression of the length to which God*
> *will go in order to restore broken community. . . . If I meet hate*
> *with hate, I become depersonalized, because creation is so*
> *designed that my personality can only be fulfilled in the context*
> *of community."*
>
> — MARTIN LUTHER KING JR.[1]

Love: The Foundation of Community

The choice of love and the accompanying perspectives of faith and hope eliminate the possibility of fear; for both cannot exist in the same person at the same time. Ambivalence or double-mindedness indicates that faith, hope, and love are not fully rooted in us at that point in time. Faith does not rely on a material outcome for verification; for it is not belief in this or that specific doctrine or manifestation. Rather, it is a fundamental experiential bond with our Creator, which connects us to the abundant life, from which nothing in life, not even the face of death, can separate us.

This is the choice we make at every moment of every day of our lives. As faith is strengthened through revelation and spiritual practice, it becomes no longer just an option, but the only way that we can be. Likewise love and hatred cannot coexist at the same moment in time, at least not the type of love to which I am referring, that is *agape* love, the unconditional love of God and our fellow human beings. Romantic love (*eros*) and affection (*philia*) can coexist with hatred, but not *agape*. Martin Luther King Jr. described it in this manner: "In speaking of love at this point, we are not referring to some sentimental emotion. . . . When we speak of loving those who oppose us, we refer to neither *eros* nor *philia*; we speak of a love that is expressed in the Greek word *agape*. *Agape* means nothing sentimental or basically affectionate; it means understanding, redeeming good will for all men, an overflowing love which seeks nothing in return. It is the love of God working in the lives of men."[2]

Fear and hatred are archaic defensive reactions that we have in common with animals. Fear is an evaluation of our external circumstances as powerful and dangerous, and ourselves as powerless, leading to the reaction of fleeing from danger. Hatred and anger flow from an evaluation of ourselves as more powerful than our perceived dangerous circumstances, leading to our reaction to fight and behave aggressively. Faith and love replace both fear and hatred through the experience of ourselves as empowered to deal with any circumstance through a spiritual bond with that which is the source off all being and creativity—God. That's why the apostle Paul can say, "I can do all things through Christ, who strengthens me."[3]

Fight or flight is our most primitive response to perceived threat, and it is still our first undisciplined reaction. But revelation and spiritual practice develop our dormant ability to respond with faith, hope, and love, rather than with fear or hatred. It is a difficult decision to make, to choose faith, because there is very real danger of loss, injury, and death in the physical world. But the decision comes with the revelation that there is also spiritual life and death, and that these are ultimately more valuable to the integrity of self and community than physical life and death.

Dr. Andrew Newberg and his colleagues have shown in their research that brain scans of people in prayer or meditation have a distinctive pattern of increased activation in the frontal lobes (associated with attention) and reduced activation in the parietal lobes (associated with orientation). This is combined with a pattern of arousal and quiescence in the autonomic nervous system. This corresponds with the combined sense of serenity and attention that is experienced by the person in prayer or meditation. They conclude: "From the neurobiological perspective, human ritual has two major characteristics. First, it generates emotional discharges, in varying degrees of intensity, that represent subjective feelings of tranquility, ecstasy, and awe; and second, it results in unitary states that, in a religious context, are often experienced as some degree of spiritual transcendence."[4]

Does the fact that biochemical changes occur during prayer mean that prayer is an addictive state that is used to escape from reality? This is not so for most people. Because prayer is tied to a moral, historical, and current system of values, responsibilities, obligations, privileges, and relationships, it is part of real life. No one has seen God, and in two thousand years, we have not been able to improve on the description that "God is spirit, and his worshippers must worship in spirit and in truth."[5] The serenity that prayer produces does not lead to isolation for most people, but rather to involvement in life with a greater focus on moral values.

Dr. Michael Persinger has used systematic application of complex electromagnetic fields to induce mystical experiences involving sensing a presence that are perceived by his subjects to be beings ranging from gods to aliens.[6] The researcher also developed a method of targeting magnetic fields via a helmet to that brain area, and inducing religious/mystical experiences in random people. It is not surprising to me that religious or mystical experiences are associated with activation of particular regions of the brain, or that activation of those regions produce the experience. The important question for me is whether being in that state gives one access to capabilities and knowledge that transcend the more usual way of being and interacting with one's environment. The researcher did reason that this capability developed in man as a survival mechanism. That is, by being able to experience themselves as part of a larger more powerful universe, our early ancestors were more cued in to dangers and possibilities in their environment, which enhanced their chances of survival.

When the apostle Paul writes about becoming a new being in Christ, he means a total transformation of a person. Today, we know that changes in thought, feeling, and behavior require corresponding changes in our brain and nervous system. Moving from a fear/hate and flight/fight response to a faith and love response similarly means making more normative the changes that Newberg and his colleagues observed in praying nuns and meditating monks. The state of alertness, relaxation, and transcendence must become our more normal state of being. It means giving spiritual life priority over material life. It means letting go and experiencing a joy and serenity that is not dependent upon our external circumstances. It is a choice that requires practice and discipline. The choice of faith and love means facing the fear of losing control (or losing the false sense of control).

The wonderful and amazing secret is that we have another way of being; that letting go of the fear does not mean we disappear, but rather we have a new life. A life where it is all right not to pretend to know and control our future, where we can freely be and become who we truly are. Once we start down that spiritual path, we must choose to continue or run back to the false safety of our fear and hatred. When we get past our fear and experience the "joy of the Lord" and the abundant life promised in the Gospel, we do not want to go back.

There will still be dry spells and challenges that separate us from the experience of the abundant life. These are the tests of faith. The redemptive message of Christianity warns us that we will not be perfected in life, but will be subject to sin and require forgiveness of each other and from God, even as we strive to live out the principles of faith and love. Even if we could totally avoid acting out of fear or hatred, we would still fall prey to acting or not acting out of indifference, which is still far removed from faith and love, and which, like all sin, separates us from God and the abundant live.

That is the central message of Christianity and other faiths that provide the capability for transformation of our personalities, our communities, and our world. Fear and hatred ultimately lead to the destruction of the self and the community, and love and faith leads to their salvation. Love leads to security and strength through unity. Fear and hatred lead to a false sense of security through domination and destruction.

Can love overcome the tendency toward abuse of power in relationships of unequal power? Perhaps the parent-child relationship is a hopeful model, though not without its own sometimes violent struggles. But for the most part, parents do not abuse the power they have over their children because they see the children as part of themselves. That perception can create its own problems, in terms of controlling the child's destiny and personality, rather than allowing him or her to flourish and develop independence. For the most part, despite what we now know about the high rates of child abuse, the relationship is benign and nurturing, rather than controlling and exploitative, or the human race would not have survived this long. Even if the biological parents are not nurturing or not available, most of us of manage to find enough nurturing from other adults to become functional human beings.

How do we get individuals, or groups of individuals, who are not related to each other, to be benign and nurturing in relationships of unequal power? The question of how we treat the poor, the orphan, and the stranger has always been a test of faith in Christianity, Judaism, and other major religions. This spirit of generosity and Godly love must be possible, or else we are doomed to a perpetual struggle for power and dominance, and the resulting violence and destruction of people, resources, and human potential.

A practical intermediate goal is to implement human social systems that seek to establish the rule of law, and attempt to balance powers against each other in order to promote justice. That is the framework we use in democratic capitalist societies. It has clearly been successful in controlling unlawful organized violence, and furthering greater tolerance of group and individual differences; but it has also created atomistic societies with widespread alienation and the loss of a sense of community and of moral values.

The healthy self only develops in relation to others, and in relation to God, where God is the ground or source of being, rather than the God of one particular religion. Without a relationship with God, our self becomes demonic. We cling to the delusion that we are God, the source and ground of being. We puff up with pride at our achievements and are obsessed with controlling and directing the world. We fixate on another person, object, or idea, and make that our God and our ultimate goal or purpose. Love, then, is the foundation of self and of community.

It is not by coincidence that Jesus reduced the original ten commandments to two fundamental ones: love of God and love of one's neighbor as oneself. A healthy self cannot develop without the loving relationship with others. We cannot become fully ourselves without that mutuality. We know this both from psychological research in child development and from our own common sense experience with children. They need to learn to love and be loved to become healthy personalities. But are we as sure about the necessity of Jesus' first commandment, to love God above all else? Can't we just learn to love each other, and develop ourselves and our community without God?

Even developing into a highly technologically advanced society has not destroyed our need for, and interest in, God. Loving God is apparently as essential to our sense of self as is the ability to love others. We cannot and do not need to prove that God exists in the same way that we exist. We can only acknowledge and testify that we need him, and that he transforms our lives. Others may see this as a weakness, or as a stage of human social evolution that will fade with even greater scientific knowledge. We can cite studies showing the positive effects of faith in overcoming illness and adversity. But ultimately, conviction comes by revelation and direct experience, not by empirical verification.

Becoming attuned to, and obeying, the will of God in our lives does not mean becoming passive and avoiding responsibility for taking action. But we cannot know the eventual outcome and total effect of our individual decisions and actions. The chain of cause and effect extends well beyond our ability to calculate. Each action could be of little or no consequence at one extreme, or at the other, it could help determine the fate of humanity. We must act not knowing where each particular action stands on a continuum of significance. Sometimes our estimates based on what we perceive and know turn out to be far off the mark. Therefore, a little humility is in order. We must humbly acknowledge our limitations and utilize all the resources available to us, even while remaining receptive to the will of God in our lives. We must listen with spiritual ears to discern the best course to take.

Repentance, Forgiveness, and Trust

Repentance and forgiveness are the rituals through which we free ourselves from the hold of the past and return to the present. Faith, or trust in God, is what allows us to stop the futile attempts to control the future and to focus on fully experiencing the present. What is the source of faith, and how do we enter into it? Faith is another way of being. With faith, we experience in the present, the resolution of all of our longings and all of our questions. It's not that we know what the future holds. Rather, it's that we experience a confidence and serenity in the present that is not dependent on external events and circumstances.

To trust in God is to let go of the fearful clinging to control, knowing that we and our world will not disappear if we do. The fear of losing control probably relates, as Erik Erikson writes, to the early childhood challenge of establishing a basic sense of trust in a nurturing parent to take care of us when we are totally helpless to do so for ourselves. As adults, we do develop, over a lifetime, tremendous power to act in the world, relative to the helpless state from which we started. Yet, as we become more aware, we see that the world is even more complicated and beyond our control, even relative to our increased capabilities. We can act, but we cannot clearly foresee the consequences of our actions, or of our inaction.

We make each decision on limited information. Trust in God means acknowledging our limitations, while still accepting responsibility for our lives. Through prayer and meditation, we connect with God, the source of creativity and being, and invite his guidance over our thoughts, words, and actions. To hear God, we must be willing to surrender our grasping for control. When we surrender, we are empowered to act with our will aligned to God's will.

We Are One

Two thousand years ago the Christian gospel proclaimed that we are all one people before God: "There is neither Jew nor Greek, slave nor free, male nor female, for you are all one in Christ Jesus. If you belong to Christ, then you are Abraham's seed, and heirs according to the promise."⁷ This made explicit the Hebrew God's promise to Abraham that "all peoples on earth will be blessed through you."⁸ Today, most of the world's population acknowledges being heirs to Abraham's covenant relationship through the religions of Christianity, Judaism, and Islam. Beyond this, we also now know scientifically that we are, in fact, one people who came from one continent, Africa, and spread out over the globe. The theory that most scientists support is that Homo sapiens appeared as a new species 150,000 to 200,000 years ago in Africa and replaced archaic humans such as Neanderthals.⁹ The minority theory is that Homo sapiens arose in Africa about two million years ago, and evolved as a single species spread out over the world, with genetic and cultural exchanges linking each region.

Not surprisingly, the seeds of human civilization, including religion, germinated and took root in the same part of the world where human beings first evolved, Africa. "It was then, on the borders of the Upper Nile, among a black race of men, that was organized the complicated system of the worship of the stars, considered in relation to the productions of the earth and the labors of agriculture . . ."¹⁰ The Bible tells us that Moses, the author and prophet of Judaism, was raised and educated as an Egyptian in Pharaoh's household. The bases he had for the foundation of Judaism as a religion and a national culture were the oral traditions of the descendants of Abraham, and the highly developed religious and scientific systems of Egypt. Both in rejecting some elements of Egyptian religion, and incorporating others, it was inevitable that the resulting product of Moses' revelation be influenced by the society in which he was raised and educated.

In the global culture of 2003, these facts would not be highly significant were it not the case that otherwise intelligent people in the United States and Europe still appear to believe that Egypt and North Africa are part of Europe or Asia, and that we in the West are heirs to a "Eurasian" civilization that includes Judaism and Christianity. The cultural contributions of Africa, Islam, pre-Columbian America, and the true Asian civilizations are trampled beneath the feet of a racial chauvinism that has lost the blunt force employed during colonization of Africa, America, and Asia, but it continues in a subtler and still poisonous form.

How do we get to the vision of a peaceful and united global community? Certainly not through the unilateral imposition of one country's, region's, or group's version of this community onto others. As I write this, the United States is involved in a military action in Iraq, against the expressed wishes of the global community, with the goal of eliminating a dictatorship we formerly supported, seizing Iraq's weapons of mass destruction (which have not been shown to exist), and spreading peace and democracy throughout the Middle East. The irony is that all of the other governments that the U.S. supports in the Middle East are dictatorships, except for Israel. And Israel appears trapped in a death spiral of aggressive colonization and brutal suppression of the Palestinians, who in turn are trapped in the politically and morally bankrupt tactic of suicide bombings against Israeli civilian targets.

Where is the vision? Political leaders and many supposedly intelligent political commentators in the U.S. appear to see the United Nations as some kind of nonessential committee, which we can ignore when we please and use when we find it convenient. To them U.S. sovereignty is paramount, and we will do whatever we see as in our national interest, regardless of the consequences to the global community. If that is true, then what is the corresponding vision of the future? Do we foresee a world in which the rest of the globe falls into line with our direction, because we are the biggest kid on the global block? Or are we still committed to universal human rights and democracy?

Ultimately, there is an essential conflict between using our military and economic muscle to enforce our version of world community against the wishes of most of the rest of the world, and the principles of human rights and democracy that we espouse. It is just as blatant as the conflict between those same principles and the system of racial discrimination that existed in this country before the civil rights movement. Dr. Martin Luther King Jr. eloquently pointed out this discrepancy and called on our country to make the right decision. We struggled with it, Dr. King and some others died for it, and eventually we made the right decision. We changed our laws and policies to match our principles.

Self-interest as a unifying principle, whether for an individual personality or for a country, has some serious limitations. It must be balanced by a willingness to see oneself through the eyes of the other, and to take action to create a community, where different unique selves and groups can find peaceful and free expression and being. Community based on the domination of the weak by the strong is inherently unstable and disingenuous. It fosters hatred and intrigue, not just among the predatory minority, who will seek unjust advantage under any circumstances, but it creates a climate of alienation that promotes Machiavellian attitudes as normative.

Power, Violence, and Nonviolence

The observation that "power tends to corrupt, and absolute power corrupts absolutely" is consistent with the Christian belief that the self is prone to pride and inflation, requiring the regular practice of humility and submission of one's will to God, in order to keep the self within proper bounds.[11] Humility is not the opposite of pride, and humility is not consistent with powerlessness in Christian belief. The apostle Paul said, "I can do all things through Christ, who strengthens me." In this conception, humility and submission to God leads to empowerment to act according to God's will in one's life. Some may confuse humility with masochism and self-debasement, but that is a misunderstanding. From the perspective of psychological and spiritual health, I put pride and sadism at one end of the continuum, and masochism and self-debasement at the other extreme.

In this sense, pride involves building up oneself by destroying or diminishing the self-hood of another person. Once the self-hood of the other person is conceptually destroyed or diminished, it is an easier next step to actually physically destroy the person, as in war or smaller violent conflicts; to use him as a beast of burden, as in slavery or labor exploitation; or to limit the other person's self-development to roles and degrees of freedom that match our own perceptions and needs, as men have historically done with women. In an odd way, this says something wonderful about us as human beings. It is not easy for us to accept ourselves as evil. In order to do evil, we usually have to develop and implement a tremendous internal and external propaganda campaign to justify harming others. As Marianne Williamson states, "No one was ever born to hate. God's love in our hearts cannot be destroyed but only temporarily put to sleep."[12] Unfortunately, we have become very good at sleeping. Humility and submission to God, leading to the empowerment of each self as unique expression of God's creativity, is the position of health, where each person can be fulfilled without needing to debase either other persons or themselves.

It is a great advance for the world when even the greatest power on earth can be to some extent checked by moral and legal constraints of the world community, as the U.S. was for a time by the United Nations in the former's rush to go to war with Iraq in 2003. Similarly within an effectively functioning democracy, the power of even the most powerful individual or group must be checked. The corruption of individual impulses of evil, that is fear, greed, pride, and hatred are not automatically countered by love. Those acting on the principle of love have to impose physical and legal constraints to control evil. Of course, those acting out of evil usually pretend to be (or even believe themselves to be) acting out of love. Thus slavery and colonialism were justified as civilizing and Christianizing the heathens. Our ability to delude ourselves about our motives sometimes seems limitless.

Those who advocate love over evil find nonviolence and peace more compatible action principles than violence and war. This principle worked at the birth of Christianity as a religion. Martyrdom and nonviolence combined with active evangelism eventually led to the establishment of Christianity as the state religion of the late Roman Empire, after which it became corrupted by its own success.

Nonviolence worked for the U.S. civil rights movement under Dr. Martin Luther King Jr., and for the Indian freedom movement under Mahatma Gandhi. But do we really believe that Hitler and the Axis powers would have been stopped by nonviolent resistance, or that the European nations would have liberated their colonies without sometimes violent resistance? Dr. King made an interesting argument that nonviolent resistance within Germany by Christians at an early stage could have prevented Hitler from implementing his demonic vision. But Dr. King was always careful to point out that nonviolence was both the most moral method, and the most practical one, for achieving equality for African-Americans.

Some people equate love with peace and nonviolence, taking an apparently consistent and principled position against the use of force under any circumstances. But even if the case can be made for the historical effectiveness of nonviolence, do we believe that civil society today can be maintained without armed police, which represent the threat and actuality of violence by the government? I think not. Even when police officers abuse their authority and brutalize innocent people, no one calls for the abolition of police forces, only better control and supervision of officers. So, while the principle of love prefers nonviolence, it cannot totally eschew the use of violence in the interest of justice. Dr. King also said, "Love is one of the pinnacle parts of the Christian faith. There is another side called justice. And justice is love in calculation. Justice is love correcting that which would work against love."[13]

While Dr. King believed in nonviolence as a principle and not simply a tactic, the reality today is that even a relatively free society requires the threat and use of state violence to maintain a semblance of justice. That should encourage us to acknowledge human corruptibility both at the level of the self, and in society, which we can transcend through a relationship with God, and control through regulation, but which, as theologian Reinhold Niebuhr discussed, we cannot totally conquer in history, either as individuals or as a community.

If we consent to society's use of violence to maintain order via a police force and a penal system, then we have to acknowledge at least this exception to a principle of nonviolence. The supreme principle is love, not peace or nonviolence. Jesus defined it as two related commandments: love of God above all else, and love of other people as we love ourselves. Under the principle of love, it is consistent to choose to allow our governments to use a legal system backed by police force and a penal system, rather than to take an absolute position against violence, and to allow the resultant chaos and greater violence. We do this even knowing that the agents of the governments will at times violate their duty and use force unjustifiably against innocent people. We work to reform the system and to institute better controls and oversight, but we do not abolish the use of force. Overall in this situation, the principle of love is more consistent with using a justice system backed by force or violence to maintain a democratic society, rather than taking a principled and absolute position against the use of violence.

If we acknowledge this exception to the principle of nonviolence, then nonviolence becomes a preferred course of action in a general sense, rather than an absolute principle. Love is the absolute principle, and at least in the case of maintaining the basic structure of a democratic society, love can justify the use of force or violence. And if the principle of love can justify the use of force under the law to maintain order in society, then there are likely other situations where the use of force between societies (war) or between groups within a society (civil war or revolution) are justifiable. Contradictions like these make living a moral life difficult. It is psychologically much simpler to take an absolutist position supporting peace and nonviolence under all circumstances, or to take the Machiavellian position that as individuals and groups, we do whatever is necessary to pursue and protect our self-interest, than to deal with all of the ambiguities and shades of gray that flow from applying the principle of love.

A Better Society

Where do we start working with the goal of creating a better society? A useful answer is to start wherever we are. Another answer is to focus on the children. If we can help more of them to become spiritually, mentally, emotionally, and physically healthy adults, then we would change the world significantly for the better. Martin Luther King Jr. had a clear vision of our problems as a global society; he saw our need of both spiritual transformation and practical economic and human rights changes in the lives of people across the globe. There are no easy answers, but there is no room for despair and hopelessness. We must all work from wherever we are at both spiritual transformation and making the world a better and more just home for humanity.

Theologian Larry Rasmussen talked about the breakdown of civil society, the organizations that provide moral guidance and a sense of unity, making community possible. "Civil society—that collection of nonmarket , nonstate communities and associations that lets people define who they are culturally and morally through mutuality and reciprocal recognition—would increasingly give way to market and state as models of society itself and as the chief moral agents of society."[14] In this "post-modern" society, there is general despair about the ability of the state and the market to sustain viable communities.

Leadership and initiatives from the faith communities and volunteers are essential, but they cannot, without the federal government, provide a program like Head Start, which supports the educational, social, psychological, and physical development of about one million poor preschool children. There are no inexpensive answers. Ultimately, we will have to choose to find ways to reduce our massive expenditures on arms and "defense" in the U.S. and other nations, in order to meet the needs for human development on a national and global basis. There is no easy way to do this either. But we will have made significant progress when politicians can no longer gain points by bragging about how much they are spending on defense. The fact that this ploy works currently is an indication of how fearful we are as a people in this country. That fear is matched by the resentment that much of the rest of the world feels toward us. They envy our technology and our wealth, and admire the democratic principles that we implement in our own country; but in our actions around the world, they frequently see our nation as a bully.

Needs and Wants

In times of need, look to the source of all creation. Experiencing lack or need, particularly by choice, can sometimes be a blessing that makes us realize our vulnerability and limitation; as well as our ability to not be spiritually bound by our physical needs, as animals are by instinct. That is probably why fasting is a traditional method of developing spiritual discipline. Psychologist Abraham Maslow talked about a "hierarchy of needs," with physical needs being the most basic, and spiritual or self-actualization needs being the highest. Sacrifice, as when a parent sacrifices her own needs in order to feed her child, or Jesus the Christ sacrificing himself for humanity, turns the hierarchy of needs upside down. The spiritual becomes more basic than the physical, and the latter can be denied even onto death.

Most of us in the U.S. and Europe do not have to choose between meeting our basic physical needs, such as for food, and meeting our spiritual needs. We do not have to sell our soul in order to eat and survive. God only knows what each of us would do if faced with that choice. For many of us, the challenge is not need, but wants and greed. The greed is sometimes symptomatic of the emptiness that physical goods cannot fill.

Sometimes believers sing and talk about a God who will give us anything we want, if we would only submit our will to his. This is fallacious if we don't understand that a relationship with God is transformational, and that our wants and even our needs are changed in the process of that relationship. Otherwise, we are really just talking about God as Santa Claus: if we appease him by being good, we will get all the goodies we want. It is understandable why God as Santa Claus is appealing and familiar in our market-oriented "post-modern" society, where we have made "the market the whole of the city, rather than one of its zones, and [subjected] all of life to the morality of the bazaar."[15] But if we do this, we really are trading our souls for a few pieces of silver. For we are giving up the power of God to transform our personalities, lives, and communities.

Freedom and Destiny

"The frequent discussion in which faith and freedom are contrasted could be helped by the insight that faith is a free, namely, centered act of the personality. In this respect freedom and faith are identical."

— PAUL TILLICH[16]

Marxists thought they could produce a secular heaven on earth by reorganizing ownership of property and of state power. But the power lust and greed that is part of human nature simply resurfaced in another form. Regulated capitalism and democracy acknowledges the primacy of selfish motivation and creates a system that allows it to flourish within constraints. The result is a society that works better economically and in terms of freedom than any known alternative. But this freedom also allows the pursuit of hedonism as well as the pursuit of the love of God. The situation is certainly not as stark as the late Roman Empire when Augustine of Hippa wrote *The City of God Against the Pagans*.[17] At that point there was no secular society, but rather a state religion of pagan gods devoid of morality.

Many decry the immorality of today's secular society compared to a nostalgic and inaccurate remembrance of a past more moral society. On a religious cable channel, a movie was recently advertised which demonstrates this type of misunderstanding about moral values in the nineteenth century compared to those of the present. The topic of the movie was how a nineteenth century man (apparently of the middle class or wealthier, as he is dressed in a nice suit) is transported to the twenty-first century, and is aghast at the decline in moral values. The apparent solution in the movie is to take the present world back to the nineteenth century. This displays the superficial view of moral values held by some members of the faith community. The nineteenth century had a view of morality that appeals to some people today because sexuality and sexual expression were repressed, and a veneer of civility and courtesy was expected in the interaction among the middle and upper class.

Meanwhile, the foundations of the society rested on slavery, sharecropping, the subjugation and exploitation of most of the world under colonialism, the unregulated exploitation of the labor of children and adults in industry and in agriculture, and the repression of women. Today, on a global basis through the United Nations, we have accepted as a norm that every person has basic human rights, and that nations have the right to self-determination.

While these rights are frequently violated, still the global understanding of what is right is accepted and has the effect of moving us (albeit slowly) toward a global goal of justice and away from the domination of the weaker by the stronger.

Some Christians decry the excesses in which many indulge now that we have a relatively free society. But it is only with freedom that each person can choose good over evil. That is the true spiritual battlefield. Therefore, for the first time in history, a large number of people on earth can make that choice. And that is good. That is God's way. "This day I call heaven and earth as witnesses against you that I have set before you life and death, blessings and curses. Now choose life, so that you and your children may live."[18]

Homophobia as Scapegoating for Heterosexual Violence and Promiscuity

> "Before they had gone to bed, all the men from every part of the city of Sodom—both young and old—surrounded the house. They called to Lot, "Where are the men who came to you tonight? Bring them out to us so that we can have sex with them." Lot went outside to meet them and shut the door behind him and said, "No, my friends. Don't do this wicked thing. Look, I have two daughters who have never slept with a man. Let me bring them out to you, and you can do what you like with them. But don't do anything to these men, for they have come under the protection of my roof."
>
> — GENESIS 19:4-8[19]

Sodom is our Western cultural archetype of the city of sexual sin and is linked, both linguistically and in common moral disparagement, to homosexuality. But the above biblical passage poses grave problems for those who use a literal interpretation of Scripture, which denies that human historical attitudes such as devaluation of women and homophobia were incorporated into the text along with the transformative message of revelation, salvation, judgment, and redemption. The "wicked thing" that Lot appears most concerned about preventing is not rape or rampant promiscuity as such, but rather homosexual activity. He is, in fact, willing to give his young daughters to the aggressive men to do with them whatever they wish, as long as his male guests are protected. The Bible says that Lot was the only righteous man to be found in Sodom. Some of our important challenges today are to separate righteousness from homophobia and the oppression of women.

Homosexuals are used by Christians morally, the way that African-Americans have historically been used by other Americans socially; as the marker, in opposition to which they can comfortably compare themselves (for example, I may be poor and ugly, but at least I'm white). Similarly, instead of acknowledging the pervasiveness of sexual promiscuity and sexual crimes in everyday heterosexual life, we focus on how homosexuals are corrupting our society and our youth. We point to scriptural support from the biblical story of Sodom and Gomorrah.

The facts are that one in three women in the U.S. is sexually abused by men. Also, explicit sexual simulation is considered normal in any film not specifically rated for children and is considered "art." These sex simulations usually add nothing to the plot or character development of the film, but give the audience the opportunity to be titillated by a quasi-pornographic display, while pretending that they are not really watching real pornography. It is also true that adultery is commonplace and visiting "strip joints" or having a female or male stripper at a party is becoming mainstream.

The Centers for Disease Control and Prevention (CDC) and the National Institute of Justice (NIJ) found in 1995–1996, that almost 25 percent of women in the U.S. report being raped and/ or physically or sexually abused by a current or former spouse, cohabiting partner, or date at some time in their lives.[20] Other studies found the prevalence to be closer to one-third of women in the U.S. and on a worldwide basis.[21] In addition, the CDC reports that the four most rigorous studies find that in 50 percent of the cases where a woman experiences intimate partner violence, her child is also abused.[22]

It seems to me that the cultural obsession with the morality of homosexuality is the equivalent of saying: "I may be unfaithful to my wife, be addicted to pornography, be a wife and/or child abuser, but at least I'm not homosexual." Next to "them," we can all feel righteous, no matter how morally depraved we really are.

God Is Good

God is the answer to two questions for which we have no answer. The first question is "Who made us?" By "us" I mean not just human beings, but the entire physical universe. Evolution tells us how life evolved on earth, but it cannot explain the origin of existence. The astrophysicists tells us about the universe beginning in a big bang fourteen billion or fifteen billion years ago, exploding from a point the size of an atom. But that does not explain how there can be a beginning, what was before the beginning, or what eternity means. It is a puzzle that defies logic. So when St. Thomas Aquinas said that for every effect, there is a cause, and God is the first cause, that is as close to a solution as any that science has been able to find so far. Science fills in important details that help us understand and manage ourselves and the resources with which we are blessed, but it cannot answer the ultimate questions.

By naming God as the creator of all things, we acknowledge him as having all power over existence and nonexistence, life and death, time and eternity, everywhere and nowhere. He is the prime mover, motivating force, and guiding principal under which all existence operates. Why do we go further and attribute self-consciousness and "personhood" to God? We recognize that God is not a physical being, that he is "a spirit, and those who worship him must worship him in spirit and in truth." But we can only relate based on what we are and what we know, so we think of God as a cosmic super-person.

Because God is powerful, that does not automatically make him good. It makes him inevitable and irresistible. Pagan gods were powerful, but amoral (or immoral) and sometimes malicious. So the other question of "What is good?" becomes important. The best answer we have been able to find in thousands of years of history is "God is good." God is good even when bad things happen to us. What if "good" and "evil" are irrelevant categories for God, and the reality simply is that "God is?" As human beings, we cannot simply "be," we have to be "good" or be "evil." Unlike animals, we can make conscious choices. And when we make a choice, we cannot just consider pleasure and pain; we must also consider good and evil. That is how we are made. And in our encounters with God, historically as described in the Bible, and today, choosing good over evil appears to us to be the paramount issue.

We know that we are weak, and that the good in us struggles with the evil, but that by ourselves, we cannot win that struggle. But thanks to God, we know, historically as well as individually, that by building a strong relationship with God through prayer, study, discipline, and fellowship, we can be better than we otherwise are, and we can create a society based on good rather than on evil. God is the mark that we strive to reach, but of which we always fall short. However, in our striving, we become better than we are. "Give thanks to the Lord, for he is good. His love endures forever."[23]

NOTES

Introduction

1. Martin Luther King Jr., "Where Do We Go From Here: Chaos or Community?", in *A Testament of Hope*, ed. James M. Washington (San Francisco: HarperSan Francisco, A Division of HarperCollins Publishers, 1986).

2. James W. Fowler, *Stages of Faith: The Psychology of Human Development and the Quest for Meaning* (San Francisco: HarperSan Francisco, A Division of HarperCollins Publishers, 1981), 17.

3. Edward P. Shafranske, ed., *Religion and the Clinical Practice of Psychology* (Washington, DC: American Psychological Association, 1996); P. Scott Richards and Allan E. Bergin, *A Spiritual Strategy for Counseling and Psychotherapy* (Washington, DC: American Psychological Association, 1997); and William R. Miller and Carl E. Thoresen, "Spirituality, Religion and Health: An Emerging Research Field," in *American Psychologist*, vol. 58, no. 1 (Washington, DC: American Psychological Association, 2003).

4. Paul Tillich, *Systematic Theology, Volume I* (Chicago: The University of Chicago Press, 1951), 110.

5. Thomas Merton, *New Seeds of Contemplation* (New York: New Directions Publishing Corporation, 1961), 14.

6. Thomas Hoyt Jr., "Testimony," in *Practicing Our Faith: A Way of Life for Searching People*, ed. Dorothy C. Bass (San Francisco: Jossey-Bass Publishers, 1997), 94.

7. Paul Tillich, *Systematic Theology, Volume I* (Chicago: The University of Chicago Press, 1951), 263-264.

8. Reinhold Niebuhr, *The Nature and Destiny of Man: A Christian Interpretation, Volume II: Human Destiny* (Louisville, Kentucky: Westminster John Knox Press, 1964), 244.

Chapter One

1. Thomas Merton, *New Seeds of Contemplation* (New York: New Directions Publishing Corporation, 1961), 30-31.

2. Romans 8:15-17, New International Version, BibleGateway.com.

3. Mark 12:30-31, New International Version, BibleGateway.com.

4. Deuteronomy 23:2, King James Version, BibleGateway.com.

5. 1 Samuel 3:10, New International Version, BibleGateway.com.

6. Matthew 7:25-27, New International Version, BibleGateway.com.

7. Francis Bacon, "De Hæresibus," *Meditationes Sacræ* (1597), cited on Quotationspage.com.

8. Proverbs 1:7, New International Version, BibleGateway.com.

9. M. Scott Peck, M.D., *The Road Less Traveled* (New York: Simon & Schuster, First Touchstone Edition, 2003).

10. Luke 12:6-7, New King James Version, BibleGateway.com.

11. John 8:3-7, New International Version, BibleGateway.com.

12. Roman 3: 23, New International Version, BibleGateway.com.

13. Paul Tillich, *Systematic Theology, Volume I* (Chicago: The University of Chicago Press, 1951), 114.

14. Abraham H. Maslow, *Religions, Values, and Peak Experiences* (New York: Penguin Books USA Inc., 1970).

15. Michael Persinger's work in the Human Consciousness Laboratory at Laurentian University, Canada, has been reported in journal articles including: Cook, C.M., and Persinger, M.A. "Experimental induction of the 'sensed presence' in normal subjects and an exceptional subject," *Percept Mot Skills* 1997 October; 85(2):683-93, and Persinger, M.A., Richards, P.M., and Koren, S.A. "Differential entrainment of electroencephalo-graphic activity by weak complex electromagnetic fields," *Percept Mot Skills* 1997 April; 84(2): 527-36.

16. Andrew Newberg, Eugene D'Aquili, and Vince Rause, *Why God Won't Go Away: Brain Science & the Biology of Belief* (New York: Ballantine Books, 2001).

17. 1 Corinthians 1:23, New International Version, BibleGateway.com.

18. Paul Tillich, *Systematic Theology, Volume I* (Chicago: The University of Chicago Press, 1951), 127.

19. Romans 8:6, New International Version, BibleGateway.com.

20. Reinhold Niebuhr, *The Nature and Destiny of Man: A Christian Interpretation, Volume II: Human Destiny* (Louisville, Kentucky: Westminster John Knox Press, 1964), 293 & 295.

21. Psalm 23:4, New International Version, BibleGateway.com.

22. Paul Tillich, *Systematic Theology, Volume I* (Chicago: The University of Chicago Press, 1951), 198.

23. Paul Tillich, *Dynamics of Faith* (New York: Harper Collins, 1957, 2001), 13.

24. Reinhold Niebuhr, *The Nature and Destiny of Man: A Christian Interpretation, Volume II: Human Destiny* (Louisville, Kentucky: Westminster John Knox Press, 1964), 304.

25. Psalm 84:10, New International Version, BibleGateway.com.

Chapter Two

1. Proverbs 11:2, New International Version, BibleGateway.com.

2. Thomas Merton, *New Seeds of Contemplation* (New York: New Directions Publishing Corporation, 1961), 200.

3. Job 6:11, New International Version, BibleGateway.com.

4. Dante Alighieri, *The Divine Comedy*, cited on Quotationspage.com.

5. Bernard Brookes, *Antisocial Attitudes, Alienation, and Rule-Breaking Behavior in Prisoners* (Boston: Boston University, doctoral dissertation, 1983).

6. Richard Christie, Florence Geis, and others, *Studies in Machiavellianism* (New York and London: Academic Press, 1970).

7. Romans 3:23, New International Version, BibleGateway.com.

8. Dante Alighieri, ibid.

9. Reinhold Niebuhr, *The Nature and Destiny of Man: A Christian Interpretation, Volume II: Human Destiny* (Louisville, Kentucky: Westminster John Knox Press, 1964), 99.

Chapter Three

1. Paul Tillich, *Systematic Theology, Volume I* (Chicago: The University of Chicago Press, 1951), 49.

2. Abraham H. Maslow, *Religions, Values, and Peak Experiences* (New York: Penguin Books USA Inc., 1970), 20.

3. M. Scott Peck, M.D., *The Road Less Traveled and Beyond* (New York: Simon & Schuster, First Touchstone Edition, 1998), 98.

4. James W. Fowler, *Stages of Faith: The Psychology of Human Development and the Quest for Meaning* (San Francisco: HarperSan Francisco, A Division of HarperCollins Publishers, 1981), 17.

5. Andrew Newberg, Eugene D'Aquili, and Vince Rause, *Why God Won't Go Away: Brain Science & the Biology of Belief*, (New York: Ballantine Books, 2001), 86.

6. Ibid., 89-90.

7. Ibid., 172.

8. Paul Tillich, *Systematic Theology, Volume I* (Chicago: The University of Chicago Press, 1951), 18.

9. Thomas Merton, *New Seeds of Contemplation* (New York: New Directions Publishing Corporation, 1961).

10. Ibid., 42.

11. *The Confessions of St. Augustine*, translated, with introduction and notes by John K. Ryan (New York: Image Books, A Division of Bantam Doubleday Dell Publishing Group, Inc., 1960).

12. Abraham H. Maslow, *Motivation and Personality*, third edition (New York: Addison Wesley Longman, Inc., 1987) and *Toward a Psychology of Being*, third edition (New York: John Wiley & Sons, Inc., 1968, 1999).

13. Paul Tillich, *Dynamics of Faith* (New York: HarperCollins, 1957, 2001), 7.

14. Romans 12:2, New International Version, BibleGateway.com.

15. 2 Peter:18-19, New International Version, BibleGateway.com.

16. Archibishop Fulton Sheen, *Life is Worth Living*, tapes and scripts of the television series are available at Catholicfamilycatalog.com.

17. *The Confessions of St. Augustine*, translated, with introduction and notes by John K. Ryan (New York: Image Books, A Division of Bantam Doubleday Dell Publishing Group, Inc., 1960), 175.

18. 1 John 2: 15-17, New International Version, BibleGateway.com.

19. *The Confessions of St. Augustine*, 104.

20. Luke 17: 20-21, New International Version, BibleGateway.com.

21. Luke 11:2, New International Version, BibleGateway.com.

22. Romans 12:2, New International Version, BibleGateway.com.

23. John 16:5-7, New International Version, BibleGateway.com.
24. Psalm 51:10-12, New International Version, BibleGateway.com.
25. Romans 10:17, New International Version, BibleGateway.com.
26. Martin Luther King Jr., "Where Do We Go From Here: Chaos or Community?", in *A Testament of Hope*, ed. James M. Washington (San Francisco: HarperSan Francisco, A Division of HarperCollins Publishers, 1986), 577-578.
27. Martin Luther King Jr., "The Trumpet of Conscience," in *A Testament of Hope*, ed. James M. Washington (San Francisco: HarperSan Francisco, A Division of HarperCollins Publishers, 1986), 644.
28. E. Durkheim, *Suicide*, translated by J.A. Spaulding and George Simpson (Glencoe, Illinois: Free Press, 1951); R. K. Merton, *Social Theory and Social Structure* (Glencoe, Illinois: Free Press, 1957); and M. Seeman, "On the Meaning of Alienation," *American Sociological Review*, 1959, 24:783-791.
29. J. Rotter, "General Expectancies for Internal Versus External Control of Reinforcement," *Psychological monographs*, 1966, 80 (1 whole no. 609).
30. Eugene Taylor, "Positive Psychology and Humanistic Psychology, A Reply to Seligman," and Kennon M. Sheldon and Tim Kasser, "Goals, Congruence, and Positive Well-Being: New Empirical Support for Humanistic Theories," in *Journal of Humanistic Psychology*, vol. 41 no. 1 (winter 2001).
31. Paul Tillich, *Systematic Theology, Volume I* (Chicago: The University of Chicago Press, 1951), 15.
32. Richard Christie, Florence Geis, and others, *Studies in Machiavellianism* (New York and London: Academic Press, 1970).

Chapter Four

1. Thomas Hoyt Jr., "Testimony," in *Practicing Our Faith: A Way of Life for Searching People*, ed. Dorothy C. Bass (San Francisco: Jossey-Bass Publishers, 1997), 99.
2. Deuteronomy 8:3, New International Version, BibleGateway.com.

Chapter Five

1. Martin Luther King Jr., "An Experiment in Love," in *A Testament of Hope*, ed. James M. Washington (San Francisco: HarperSan Francisco, A Division of HarperCollins Publishers, 1986), 20.

2. Martin Luther King Jr., "Nonviolence and Racial Justice," in *A Testament of Hope*, ed. James M. Washington (San Francisco: HarperSan Francisco, A Division of HarperCollins Publishers, 1986), 8.

3. Philippians 4:13, New King James Version, BibleGateway.com.

4. Andrew Newberg, Eugene D'Aquili, and Vince Rause, *Why God Won't Go Away: Brain Science & the Biology of Belief* (New York: Ballantine Books, 2001), 86.

5. John 4:24, New International Version, BibleGateway.com.

6. Michael Persinger's work in the Human Consciousness Laboratory at Laurentian University, Canada, has been reported in journal articles including: Cook, C.M., and Persinger, M.A., "Experimental induction of the 'sensed presence' in normal subjects and an exceptional subject," *Percept Mot Skills* 1997 October; 85(2):683-93, and Persinger, M.A., Richards, P.M., and Koren, S.A. "Differential entrainment of electroencephalo-graphic activity by weak complex electromagnetic fields," *Percept Mot Skills* 1997 April; 84(2):527-36.

7. Galatians 3:28-29, New International Version, BibleGateway.com.

8. Genesis 12:3, New International Version, BibleGateway.com.

9. Kate Wong, "The Modern Human Origins Morass," *Scientific American*, January 29, 2001.

10. C.F. Volney, quoted in John G. Jackson's *Introduction to African Civilizations* (New York: Citadel Press, Kensington Publishing Corp., 2001).

11. Quote attributed to Lord Acton, 1887, Quotationspage.com.

12. Marianne Williamson, *Everyday Grace* (New York: Riverhead Books, Penguin Putnam, Inc., 2002), 42.

13. From Martin Luther King Jr.'s "Holt Street Address," cited in James H. Cone, *Risks of Faith: The Emergence of Black Liberation Theology 1968-1998* (Boston: Beacon Press, 1999), 67.

14. Larry L. Rasmussen, *Moral Fragments & Moral Community: A Proposal for Church in Society* (Minneapolis: Augsburg Fortress, 1993).

15. Ibid., 67-68.

16. Paul Tillich, *Dynamics of Faith* (New York: HarperCollins, 1957, 2001), 6.

17. Augustine, *The City of God Against the Pagans*, ed. R. W. Dyson (Cambridge, UK: Cambridge University Press, 1998).

18. Deuteronomy 30:19, New International Version, BibleGateway.com.

19. Genesis 19:4-8, New International Version, BibleGateway.com.

20. The Centers for Disease Control and Prevention and The National Institute of Justice, *Extent, Nature, and Consequences of Intimate Partner Violence*, Atlanta, Georgia: July 2000.

21. L. Heise, M. Ellsberg, and M. Gottemoeller, *Ending Violence Against Women*. Population Reports, Series L, No. 11, December 1999.

22. The Commonwealth Fund, *Health Concerns Across a Woman's Lifespan: 1998 Survey of Women's Health*, May 1999; and The Centers for Disease Control and Prevention, *Co-occurrence of Intimate Partner Violence Against Mothers and Abuse of Children*, Fact Sheet, Atlanta, Georgia: 2002.

23. Psalm 136:1, New International Version, BibleGateway.com.

INDEX

INDEX

Faith 125, 126, 129, 131
and setbacks 98
purpose of 11
tests of 129, 130
Fasting 140
Fear 54, 57, 67, 68, 69, 103, 104,
111, 125, 126, 129, 136
letting go of 128
of death 57
Forgiveness 18, 131–32
Fowler, James 92
Frankle, Victor 95
Free will 146
Freedom 63, 142–43
Freud, Sigmund 94, 95, 107, 110
concept of projection 112

Gambling 102
Gandhi, Mahatma 137
Geis, Florence 84
Greed 57, 104, 136, 141

Habit 103, 106
and addiction 102
and sin 94
Hatred 57, 103, 111, 129, 135,
136
coexisting with love 126
Hierarchy of needs 96, 110, 140
and sacrifice 140
Hitler, Adolf 137
Holy Spirit 86, 99, 105, 115
Homosexuality 143–45
Hope 86
Hoyt, Thomas, Jr. 113

Human personality
Freud conception of 94, 110
Greek conception of 93, 100
Humanistic psychology 95, 109
Humility 57, 111, 131, 135

Immorality
today vs. yesterday 142–43
Immortality 75
Indifference 129
Insecurity 103
Iraq War 134, 136
Islam 133

Jesus Christ 105
sacrifice of 104
Job, book of 98
Judaism 133
Jung, Karl 95
Justice 108, 130, 137

Kelleher, Philip 73
Kennedy, Robert 120
King, Martin Luther, Jr. 108,
120, 125, 126, 135, 137, 139
Kingdom of God
coming of 105
Kirk, Rahsaan Roland 72, 121

Laws, Hubert 121, 122
Learned helplessness 109, 110,
112
Love 111, 125–31, 136
and power 108
applying the principle of 137
of God 115, 126, 130–31, 138

155

ABOUT THE AUTHOR

DR. BERNARD BROOKES is president and cofounder of BHM International, Inc., a consulting firm that provides technical assistance and training in health, education, and other human services to nonprofit organizations. He is also cofounder and former executive director of the Center for Health and Development, a mental health service agency in Massachusetts. Prior to working independently, Dr. Brookes was affiliated with Harvard Medical School and McLean Hospital as a clinical fellow in psychology, an instructor in psychology, and a clinical unit director at Bridgewater State Hospital in Massachusetts. He is a former treasurer of the Massachusetts Psychological Association and a member of the American Psychological Association. He earned a bachelor degree in music at Berklee College, master's and doctoral degrees in clinical and community psychology at Boston University, and a master's of business administration degree also at Boston University. He is president of the Health Ministry and a trustee of Poplar Grove Baptist Church in Maryland.